John Quincy Adams

Experiences of the Higher Christian Life in the Baptist Denomination

being the testimony of a number of ministers and private members of Baptist churches to the reality and blessedness of the experience of sanctification

John Quincy Adams

Experiences of the Higher Christian Life in the Baptist Denomination

being the testimony of a number of ministers and private members of Baptist churches to the reality and blessedness of the experience of sanctification

ISBN/EAN: 9783337159580

Printed in Europe, USA, Canada, Australia, Japan

Cover: Foto ©Lupo / pixelio.de

More available books at **www.hansebooks.com**

EXPERIENCES

OF THE

HIGHER CHRISTIAN LIFE

IN THE

BAPTIST DENOMINATION;

BEING THE

TESTIMONY OF A NUMBER OF MINISTERS AND PRIVATE MEMBERS OF BAPTIST CHURCHES TO THE REALITY AND BLESSEDNESS OF THE EXPERIENCE OF SANCTIFICATION, THROUGH FAITH IN THE BLOOD OF JESUS CHRIST.

EDITED BY JOHN Q. ADAMS,

AUTHOR OF "BAPTISTS THOROUGH RELIGIOUS REFORMERS," "SANCTIFICATION," "FULL SALVATION," "VESSEL UNTO HONOR," ETC., ETC.

NEW YORK:
SHELDON & COMPANY, 500 BROADWAY.
BOSTON: GOULD & LINCOLN.
CHICAGO: S. C. GRIGGS & CO.

1870.

PREFACE.

About ten years ago there appeared a remarkable book, entitled "The Higher Christian Life," written by Rev. W. E. Boardman, the design of which was to direct the attention of Christians of all denominations to a phase of religious experience known to comparatively few, and yet the exalted privilege of all the redeemed family of Christ. The peculiar excellence of that work consisted in explaining and harmonizing the different, and, in some instances, apparently conflicting terms, employed to set forth that experience, and the adoption of a new phrase, which derived its significance and force from its comparative, rather than its absolute form. That which Methodists had designated "Christian perfection" or "perfect love," Oberlin teachers "entire sanctification" or "perfection," Presbyterians, Baptists and others "full assurance of faith" or the "rest of faith," was here denominated "The Higher Christian Life"—a phrase which, while it indicated the enjoyment of the comparative, did not claim the possession of the superlative, in Christian attainment.

One of the exceedingly happy results accomplished by the wide circulation of this work was its tendency to remove prejudice, and excite calm inquiry as to the possibility of reaching a better phase of religious life, and, in many instances, inspiring the earnest and successful effort to gain a higher and sweeter experience of Jesus' power and love.

Its unsectarian character gave it favor among all denominations of Christians; and, among all, God has signally blessed it. To many it came as a special messenger from God, sent just in the time of need, to aid and encourage them in their struggles against sin and their yearnings for triumph over the corruptions of their depraved nature.

Above all, the clearness with which the author demonstrated, from the Word of God, the necessity of such an experience and the provisions made for its permanent possession, gave it a peculiar power with those who demand a "Thus saith the Lord" for all they receive as doctrine or precept in religious matters. Among these we class especially and pre-eminently Baptists. Turning away from the uncertain voice of Tradition in all spiritual concerns, and adhering to God's Word, they demand that all things be brought to this test, and fearlessly reject any and all theories, experiences, and practices that do not harmonize with the teachings of the Holy Spirit. Hence their great inquiry ever has been, "What saith the Scriptures?" On the subject of the "Higher Life," Mr. Boardman's work seemed to answer this question conclusively, and many in this denomination who had already been led by the teaching of the Word and Spirit of God into the experience of this grace, were emboldened openly to testify to the possession of it, while many others were led to seek and obtain it.

A periodical "devoted to the advancement of Gospel Holiness" was published by the editor of this book, and soon became a bond of union among a large number who, by Divine grace, walked in the higher life. In this periodical many of the experiences in the following pages were first published, while others are here presented for the first time.

It has not been thought advisable in all instances to give the *names* of the writers, but the reader may be assured that each experience was written by a member "in good standing and full fellowship" in some Baptist church, as his or her testimony to the power of Jesus fully to save. The design of their publication is to encourage and help others who are struggling after this higher life, and to awaken a deeper and more general interest on the subject of holiness in our beloved denomination, and among all the redeemed family of God.

Let it be specially noticed that these experiences are related by persons in all stations and conditions in life—thus proving that all the blessings of the new covenant may be enjoyed by any child of God, however prominent or obscure his station, or however exalted or depressed his condition.

In the martyr-days of the Baptist denomination, holiness of heart and purity of life were as prominent characteristics among us as earnest zeal for the Scriptural observance of gospel ordinances. God grant that in these days the latter may not outrun the former, but that both may be united as the legitimate fruit of the "Higher Christian Life."

J. Q. A.

New York, 1870.

CONTENTS.

                                                                PAGE
EXPERIENCE I.
Miss S. M. G., Teacher in a Public School in New York
City... 11

EXPERIENCE II.
Rev. Elihu Gunn Pastor in Iowa...................... 26

EXPERIENCE III.
Miss ——, Teacher in a Brooklyn Mission.............. 38

EXPERIENCE IV.
Miss C. W., of New York City........................ 42

EXPERIENCE V.
R. A. S., a Brother in Indiana....................... 52

EXPERIENCE VI.
Mrs. A. S.. 57

EXPERIENCE VII.
A Struggling Pastor.................................. 66

EXPERIENCE VIII.
O. A., a Norwegian Sailor............................ 75

EXPERIENCE IX.
Miss J. F. T.... 82

EXPERIENCE X.
Miss C. R., of New York City.......................... 92

EXPERIENCE XI.
Rev. A. P. Graves, the Evangelist..................... 109

EXPERIENCE XII.
Mrs. J. H.. 120

EXPERIENCE XIII.
Rev. John Q. Adams, Pastor in New York City.......... 126

EXPERIENCE XIV.
Mrs. A. H... 147

EXPERIENCE XV.
Rev. C. W. Brooks, Pastor in Broome County, N. Y...... 160

EXPERIENCE XVI.
Mrs. E. P. G....................................... 171

EXPERIENCE XVII.
Rev. J. J. M., Pastor in Massachusetts.................. 175

EXPERIENCE XVIII.
Mrs. L. J. H....................................... 182

EXPERIENCE XIX.
Rev. D. B. Gunn, Pastor in Illinois.................... 186

EXPERIENCE XX.
Mrs. S. S., of New York City.............. 196

EXPERIENCE XXI.
Rev. R. B. Andrews, Pastor in Maine................... 205

EXPERIENCE XXII.
Miss M. H., of Cortland Co., N. Y...................... 209

EXPERIENCE XXIII.
Rev. —— —— ——, Baptist Minister in Kansas......... 211

EXPERIENCE XXIV.
Mrs. H. A. Parker...................................... 221

EXPERIENCE XXV.
Rev. W. E. Noyes, Pastor in Maine.................... 225

EXPERIENCE XXVI.
Mrs. M. A. T... 230

EXPERIENCE XXVII.
Rev. G. F. Pentecost, Pastor in Brooklyn, N. Y.......... 234

EXPERIENCE XXVIII.
Mrs. E. W. T... 236

EXPERIENCE XXIX.
J. H. S., of New Haven, Conn.......................... 242

EXPERIENCE XXX.
L. R., a brother in Indiana............................ 248

EXPERIENCE XXXI.
Mrs. H. A. R.. 256

EXPERIENCE XXXII.
Miss Lizzie M... 264

EXPERIENCE XXXIII.
L. M. W., Steward of the "Band of Faith" in Shurtleff College, Ill.. 269

EXPERIENCE XXXIV.
Mrs. C. H. Putnam, a Member of the First Baptist Church, New York City... 271

EXPERIENCE XXXV.
A Pastor's Wife.. 281

EXPERIENCE XXXVI.
Mrs. M. A. S... 284

HIGHER LIFE EXPERIENCES.

EXPERIENCE OF MISS S. M. G.,

TEACHER IN A PUBLIC SCHOOL IN NEW YORK CITY.

WHEN about the age of seven, I was led to see that I was a sinner in the sight of God, and that I never could go to heaven with such a wicked heart. I was deeply troubled for some time. I often went alone and asked God to give me a new heart, and make me like Jesus. Being naturally very diffident, I did not speak of my feelings to any one, and the deep anxiety I then felt gradually wore off, though the truth then so deeply impressed on my mind that I "must be born again," never entirely left me. I was very lively, and nothing seemed for any length of time to depress my spirits. I always attended Sunday-school, went to church regularly, read the Bible, said my prayers every night, and once in a while in the morning, never went to the theatre, ball-room, or any such place, and thought myself as good as the majority of professed Christians. And though, deep within my heart, was the consciousness that I "must be born again," yet my proud spirit would not admit it; and so I went on, vainly trying to persuade myself that I could gain heaven by my good works. Thus I continued until I was about fourteen years of age.

The church of which my parents were members, and where I was in the habit of attending, had been for some time without a pastor; but, about this time, God sent one through whom he designed I should learn the way to himself. Oh! how often have I praised the Lord for sending him just at that time, and how clearly I now see the hand of my heavenly Father gently leading me to himself. When he first came I took no interest in the preaching, for I was beginning to feel very careless and indifferent about eternal things; but, on the third Sunday in January, 1856, he preached a sermon from the words: "The harvest is past, the summer is ended, and we are not saved."

I had not entered the church with any desire to

be benefited, but simply because it had become a habit; so that I did not give any particular attention to the services. As soon, however, as the text was announced, my attention was drawn to the sermon, and I listened very attentively for some minutes, when, to my utter surprise, I found the minister was talking about me. He was telling the people all about me, just as well—yea, far better than I could have told it. Oh! how mortified I felt. I covered my face with my hand, and wished I could get out without any one seeing me. I could only think of one person to whom I had given the least intimation of the state of my mind; so I supposed, of course, she had gone to him and told him all she knew about me, and, between them, they had guessed out the rest. Oh! how angry I felt at her for telling him, and at him for repeating it before the whole congregation.

By the time the services were ended, I had made up my mind never again to enter that church; but, when it was time for the evening meeting, I seemed to be drawn by an irresistible power to the sanctuary. I could not stay home, and I went to the meeting. It was a prayer-meeting, and was very solemn. Each one who spoke or prayed made some reference to the judgment-day, when the harvest would indeed be ended, and the summer gone. Then a brother started the hymn:

> "Oh! there will be mourning
> At the judgment-seat of Christ."

I did not then know that the Spirit of God was striving with me. I thought that all the members of the church, with the pastor, had joined together to frighten me into religion. I thought I would keep away from them; but this proved impossible, for every time the sanctuary was opened for worship I was there.

And now my trouble was, I could not *feel*. I knew I was a sinner—I had known this all my life—but I could not feel; and I was very much afraid these impressions would wear off, and leave me as I was before. I went to church regularly, read the Bible, and tried to pray; but I only grew worse. I remember one night I felt so discouraged, I thought it was of no use for me to try any longer. Satan suggested that I was only making myself miserable and unhappy, when there was no need of it; I was quite young, and had many years to live yet; and so I prepared to retire. I was just about to place my head upon the pillow, when these words seemed to be spoken by an audible voice: "Thou fool, this night thy soul shall be required of thee." I started up with fear and alarm. It was in the month of February; a cold, frosty night; the moon was shining brightly, making the room light. I looked around; no one was there. I went to the window and opened it, that the cold air might fan my fevered brow. Oh, what anguish my soul was in! I felt—yes, I was brought to feel —that I was the *chief of sinners;* I felt that I did not deserve the mercy of God, and that he would be just if he should cast me off for ever. I no longer thought myself as good as others; oh, no! my self-righteousness was all gone. For a week or two after this, I felt as if no man cared for my soul. No sermon seemed to reach my case, for, when the minister would preach to "anxious sinners," I thought I was not anxious enough to claim the message.

Thus Satan kept me from receiving any comfort or instruction from the Word preached. I was truly miserable. I felt that the wrath of God had been kindled against me, and I did not know at what moment I should be cast down to hell. I could not murmur or complain, for I felt it would be right; but oh, I prayed that God would, for Jesus' sake, have mercy upon me, though I was the greatest sinner on the earth.

In the month of March I called to see my pastor, with an earnest desire to be directed to Christ, and, though my load of sin was not removed, I returned home determined to find Christ or perish—resolved that if I did perish, it should be at Jesus' feet. My proud nature was humbled, and I was willing now to come to Jesus, and be saved by him alone. And yet, for a month longer I struggled and prayed, and then called on the pastor a second time. And then, oh! amazing love; my Jesus came so near! He spake words of tenderness and love, to soothe my anguished heart, and filled my soul with peace. A load like a mountain seemed to roll off my heart, and I felt as light and free as a bird. We were kneeling at the time, and the pastor was praying. I did not seem to hear his voice; I forgot everything about me. But I was brought to a consciousness of where I was, by hearing him use in his prayer the very language my soul was uttering: "My Beloved is mine, and I am His." In what connection he used the quotation, I did not know.

On rising from my knees I fixed my eyes on one of the window-shades, on which was painted Jesus blessing little children. I thought if I should take my eyes off that shade, or even move, the sweet peace I then had would pass away and leave me as

I was before. My pastor asked me if I now thought Jesus was willing to save me. I felt afraid to answer, lest this peace which had taken possession of my soul should vanish. But when he asked me if I loved Jesus, my heart gave a bound, and I answered earnestly: "*I do; he is my Saviour.*" I had no ecstatic or rapturous emotions, but a calm, peaceful delight; a resting in Jesus as my Saviour, my Redeemer. Oh! how unworthy I felt—deeply realizing that it was all of grace. How changed everything appeared. The sun seemed to shine with renewed splendor; every one I met seemed to be smiling; the Word of God was a new book, and prayer was a delight. On the first Sunday in May I was baptized and received into the North Baptist Church of New York city.

It now was my earnest desire to follow Christ, and serve him faithfully all my days. I found, from the Word of God, that I was not to be conformed to this world; I was to be different in every respect. I loved Jesus with all my heart, and it was an easy thing to obey all his commands, to follow all his precepts. The worship of God was my delight, and never was I absent from the sanctuary if it was possible for me to be present. While I attended the outward means of grace, private devotion was not neglected. It was here that Jesus revealed himself more peculiarly to my soul, and held sweet communion with me.

For some time I enjoyed almost uninterrupted peace and nearness to Christ—then came a season of darkness. I could not understand it. I thought Jesus had left me, and that I had never been converted; but God was teaching me that I must not depend upon my feelings. He had something better for me than that; and was even then leading me to trust fully in him. But oh, what a slow learner I have been! How often has God had to give me the same lesson, over and over again. Truly, with me it has been "precept upon precept, precept upon precept, line upon line, line upon line, here a little, and there a little." I felt that I could not live without Christ; and I saw, now, the utter inability of all earthly things to satisfy one whose eyes had been opened to view him, who is "altogether lovely," and the "chiefest among ten thousand." My earnest cry was: "Take what thou wilt, Lord; but oh, give me Jesus." "Restore unto me the joys of thy salvation." My heavenly Father heard the cry of his child, and enabled me again to rejoice in the light of his countenance.

Thus two years passed; at times I enjoyed much

of the presence of Christ, and then, for days and weeks I would be shut up in the deepest cell of "Doubting Castle." But, at all times, I had an earnest, anxious desire to be entirely conformed to Christ—to be as much like Jesus as it was possible for me to be. I prayed for a closer walk with God; I asked him to make me a true, whole-hearted Christian. He was answering my prayer, and leading me nearer himself, but in a way I did not expect. The language of the 43d hymn in the supplement to the Psalmist, commencing—

"I asked the Lord that I might grow
In faith and love, and every grace,"

seemed to be my experience. God answered my prayer by leading me through trials, temptations, and afflictions. I was a very desponding Christian, and often went with my head bowed down like a bulrush. Oh, surely, this was not recommending the religion of Jesus Christ to the world. I felt this keenly, but did not know how to remedy it. How my soul longed to know more of Jesus! How earnestly I prayed that I might grow in grace, and become established and settled in Christ; for I felt like a wave of the sea, tossed by every passing breeze. Oh, how I "hungered and thirsted after righteousness;" but I was told I must not expect to be satisfied in this life. So, in prospect of enduring these yearnings all my life, I became weary, oh, *so* weary and tired of living, that I would often ask God to take me to himself.

During the fall of 1858, I was laid upon a bed of sickness. I had been sick several times since my conversion, and, on each occasion, Jesus seemed very precious. At one time I seemed to be on the very brink of the grave. My soul was filled with rapture; I was exceedingly happy; for I thought I was going home. And the thought that seemed to inspire my soul with heavenly joy was: *there is no sin there.* But, when I was told I would live, how disappointed I felt! I was not willing that God should have his way. I could not say, "Thy will be done;" for my will had not yet been brought into harmony with the Divine will. During the sickness of which I am about to speak, Jesus did not reveal himself so fully to my soul as on former occasions, and this led me to serious reflection and self-examination.

One day when my pastor came to see me, he told me he thought I was becoming sick of self. After he left me I thought much of what he had said, and asked Jesus to show me more of my own heart —that he would let me see myself, in some degree at least, as he saw me. Oh! what a sight I beheld, when, in answer to prayer, Jesus permitted me to see something of my own depravity! I loathed and abhorred myself, as I never did before.* But, strange to say (at least it seemed strange to me), I did not become desponding and think I never was converted; but the Spirit of God directed my mind to the prayer of the Psalmist: "Create in me a *clean* heart, O God, and renew a right spirit within me." When I recovered from this sickness, I went to my pastor and told him the state of my mind, asking him what I should do. But to my surprise he told me he could not tell me; he did not know what advice to give, as he himself was in the same state of mind. However, he lent me a book, entitled, "The Higher Christian Life." I read it with much delight, for I found there *were* some who enjoyed just the experience for which my soul longed. I learned that sanctification was a distinct work of grace, performed by the Spirit of God in the heart of the believer.

I now began to search the Word of God more carefully and prayerfully than I had ever done before. I wanted to know what the Bible taught on this subject, and I found an experience spoken of there, above everything I had ever known, and which I had previously thought was confined to the apostles and early Christians; or, if it was enjoyed by Christians in the present time, it was after they had grown up into it. But now my eyes were opened, and I saw it was the privilege of every believer; and more than this, it was constantly urged upon them by the apostles. I determined, by the help of God, to seek this experience.

In order to have Jesus take up his abode in my heart, to abide with me, I found from the Word of God, and the work I have alluded to, that I must surrender myself entirely to God; that I must present myself "a living sacrifice," to be used by my heavenly Father as he should see fit. In accordance with this conviction, I wrote out a full consecration, and signed it.

I now thought I had done all that was required of me, but I failed in a very important part: I did not, I *could* not *believe* that God would accept such an unworthy offering. For nearly a year I waited, looking for something more to add to the offering, and acting as if I expected to find some worthiness in myself.

On the first day of January, 1860, being Sunday, my pastor, having himself experienced entire sanctification, preached from the words: "And they began, on the first day of the first month, to sanctify." I was led, by the Spirit of God, to cast myself on the altar of sacrifice, to renew my consecration, and believe that God did accept me, for Christ's sake. Satan, as usual, was busy; when he found he was about to lose me, he redoubled his efforts. He told me I was not *all* given up, there was something I had held back; I then said, "Lord, I give thee *all*—known or unknown."

Among other things, Satan told me I was too unworthy; God could not accept such an offering. Oh, how strong was this temptation! He brought to my mind the Jewish offerings; they must be without spot or blemish, and could I think God would accept me, in all my vileness and unworthiness? Reason answered, "No; Jesus *never* will condescend to take up his abode in your heart." But the Holy Spirit whispered: "Accepted in the Beloved;" "The altar sanctifieth the gift;" "Only believe;" "All things are possible to him that believeth." I then said, "I *will* believe." But this was not enough—I was to believe *now*. It seemed to me a desperate effort. I had no emotional change; I did not feel different. And on this point Satan tempted me sorely. But, with the help of the Spirit, I exclaimed, "I *do* believe." The Lord saw fit to lead me some time by simple faith—a childlike dependence on the Word of God. And then, when I was emptied of self, I was filled with glory and with God. For the first time in my life, my soul was continually satisfied. My need was all supplied. Oh, the fulness of Jesus! I was saved, fully saved from sin.

Years have passed since I received from the Lord the blessing I sought of him—entire sanctification. During that time, oh, what a change has taken place in me. I am no longer the desponding, unhappy creature I was. I do not now grow weary of life. I love to have the *will of God done;* and as long as he sees fit to keep me here, I am willing to stay. Surely, I am a wonderful "miracle of grace." The Lord has indeed done great things for *me,* whereof I am glad. I have often thought I was a poor, unworthy creature, but I have never known my unworthiness as I know it now. Oh, how I have been led to loathe myself; and how I have sunk in self-abasement at the foot of the cross, completely overwhelmed with a view of self. And oh, how sweet to have Jesus take me, and wash me in his own precious blood, and realize that I am cleansed. Oh, how fully Jesus does save.

My greatest desire now, is to live for Jesus; to

glorify him by my looks, my actions, my walk, and even the tones of my voice. I am led to see my own weakness more and more each day, and this leads me to look to Jesus each moment. And when, in view of my vileness, I am led to exclaim:

> "Every moment, Lord, I need,
> The merit of Thy death,"

I can, by divine grace, triumphantly add:

> "Every moment, Lord, I *have*
> The merit of Thy death.

I am, indeed,

> "A poor sinner, and nothing at all,
> But Jesus Christ is my all in all."

EXPERIENCE OF ELIHU GUNN,

A BAPTIST PASTOR IN IOWA.

I CANNOT remember the time when I was not the subject of occasional deep religious impressions. The loss of a pious mother, when I was nine years of age, threw a tinge of sadness over all my early years, and doubtless very deeply affected all my subsequent religious history. At thirteen years of age, I was deeply convicted of sin, during the prevalence of a powerful revival of religion. It was not, however, until I was twenty-one years old, that any permanent change was wrought upon me. At that time, I have always thought, God gave me a new heart, although my evidences of the change were far from being as clear and satisfactory as they should have been. I waded for months, the most of the time through darkness and doubt, and did not "put on Christ" till nearly a year after. My view of Christ as a Saviour was exceedingly imperfect, and of course my realizations of his grace were very few and small. After uniting with the church, however, I made considerable advancement, and at times enjoyed intimate communion with the Saviour.

About this time a circumstance occurred to me, which greatly changed my whole subsequent religious life. I became, for the first time, acquainted with the doctrine of sanctification, through some persons who held the views on that subject, taught at Oberlin. My mind was greatly interested upon the subject. I read "Mahan on Christian Perfection," and other similar publications, and endorsed the doctrine fully. Now began a struggle in my mind, which continued twenty years, and which, in painful, agonizing intensity, it is beyond my feeble powers to describe. I obtained pretty clear views of the extent of the claims of God's law, and heinous nature of sin, while I did not obtain a corresponding view of Jesus as a Saviour—at least as *my* Saviour—from the guilt of sin, and the curse and condemnation of the law. My conscience was enlightened, but my will was enslaved. How often I read the burning words of Paul, in the seventh of Romans, and applied them all to myself.

Not knowing Christ as a Saviour from sin, my

refuge must be, of course, myself; my own strength —my own resolutions. I was a slave to sin; from that bitter bondage I must be free. I *would* be free. Tears and groans almost innumerable I poured forth. Often I fasted and afflicted my soul. I struggled with my chain, but could not break it. Resolutions I made, in almost every form. Alas! they were powerless, as a bank of sand against the mighty rushing of the cataract. Once, I opened a vein in my arm, and wrote a vow in my own blood. I soon broke the vow, and then burned it. Scores of times did I repeat: "I am carnal, sold under sin. Who shall deliver me from the body of this death?" How strange it now seems to me that I did not know how to say: "I thank God, through Jesus Christ our Lord."

Sometimes I would get a temporary victory over certain forms of sin, which would give me a gleam of comfort and hope, but it was only lopping off the branches, or at most cutting down the trunk of the deadly upas tree, while the roots remained in a fruitful soil, to send forth a new growth of poisonous shoots. This was my prevailing, not my uniform, state of mind. Through all those years, there were occasional intervals like gleams of sunshine through dark clouds, when I found it sweet to hold communion with the Saviour, and could sing of his delivering grace and mercy. But, ordinarily, it was bondage—bitter, galling, degrading bondage—to sin and Satan. I read the pungent words of the Saviour: "Whosoever committeth sin is the slave (*doulos*) of sin;" and I did not need any confirmation of their truth, for I had a bitter confirmation in my daily and hourly experience.

After several years spent in this way, seeking for deliverance from sin, and the sanctification of my heart, I finally became discouraged, and concluded that entire sanctification could not be secured in this life. My mind had become too much enlightened on the subject, however, to be satisfied with the old and prevalent view, that there is no such thing as deliverance from the dreadful bondage of sin, until the hour and article of death; and that the very highest type of Christian experience is that described by Paul in the seventh of Romans. My mind settled down in about this position: There is a "higher Christian life." What the Oberlin and Methodist brethren call "Christian perfection," "entire sanctification," etc., has a real existence; but they err in the names they give it; and perhaps, also, in calling it a full deliverance from sin.

I was now pursuing a course of study for the ministry, and theological questions must be settled. But the settling of theological questions did not bring quiet to the heart. There the war raged with all its former bitterness and fury. I was a slave to sin, and Christ had died to set me free. Two hostile powers were contending within my soul: sin and holiness were arrayed against each other, and extermination must take place with the one or the other before that contest could end. I do not overdraw this picture—it is hardly possible to overdraw it. I peruse my diary, written during all the long weary months of that eight years' course of study and preparation for the ministry, with utter astonishment now. "How is it possible," I exclaim, "that I should have been so blind? And why did not some one, who knew better, show me the way of deliverance?"

My course completed, I settled in life, and took the pastoral charge of a church. For a time I enjoyed more spiritual light. I devoted myself earnestly to the work, and the blessing of God attended. Revivals followed, and sinners were converted. I was, however, painfully conscious that there was a sad lack in my preaching—a want of living power. Pride and self had a large place in all that I did. In my pulpit performances I was elated by success, or depressed by failure; and I well knew that unholy ambition was the ruling motive in much that I did. Much of the time I did not enjoy religion. Often I used to say that I felt infinitely dissatisfied with my religious experience. I was in profound darkness, and I knew it; but how to get out, I could not tell. I knew that Christ was the only Saviour, and I believed that he was an all-sufficient Saviour; but I could not lay hold of him, to be delivered from sin. Pride, and ambition, and a host of other lusts, festered in my heart, and I could not drive them out. Strange, that I did not apply to the One "stronger than they."

At length God laid his hand upon me. My pride was humbled. My wealth, in which I had trusted, was all taken from me. My ambitious schemes were all thwarted, and my brightest prospects blasted. The storm that passed over me laid me low, but it cleared the atmosphere around, and gave me to see more fully where I stood. I heard a voice saying to me: "Seekest thou great things for thyself? Seek them not." I was made willing to be little and despised. A great change had come over me, and yet not the change which I desired. I was not yet delivered from the thraldom of sin.

About this time, in the providence of God, I

changed my field of labor, and was brought into association with a number of dear Christian friends, who enjoyed the blessing of "perfect love," and were living witnesses of its preciousness and power. It was the first time in my life that I had been thus privileged. I found companionship with such spirits sweet, but my own mind was not particularly interested in the subject, until one day, conversing with a dear brother, a Baptist minister, I told him I did not think the attainment of entire sanctification possible in this life. To my surprise he replied: "I am persuaded that it is. I examined the subject years ago, and I think that our Methodist brethren are right in their views upon it."

God made these words like a prophet's voice to my heart. Instantly I said to myself: "I will now settle that question in my own mind. I will know if Christ has provided such a blessing for his people, and promised it to them." I read God's word with earnest prayer, and availed myself of such help as came within my reach. No great amount of time was requisite to bring my mind to a full decision. I was somewhat familiar with the subject, and I found too much Scripture testimony to allow me to doubt. I said: "This is the truth of God—this is the promised inheritance of every believer." Another decision, just as instantaneous, and just as emphatic, was now made: "This blessing is for all—it is for *me*. By the grace of God I will have it." At once I set myself to use all the means in my power. I sought light from every source. I desired to know precisely what was the blessing promised, and how it was to be secured. On both these points I soon obtained much clearer light than ever I had possessed before.

I was willing to receive instruction from any source. Gladly would I sit at the feet of the humblest disciple, if he could point me to the way of holiness. Sectarian epithets had lost all their terror, and I was willing to be called by any name, if I could be freed from the terrible thraldom of sin, under which I had groaned for more than twenty years. I felt that I should be delivered, and promised God that if he would give me this great light, I would strive to let it shine to all around. I prayed for a *clear* experience, in order that I might be able the better to assist others into the way, when I should become established in it. I saw clearly that I was required to "come out from among them, and be separate;" to "present my body, a living sacrifice, holy and acceptable to God;" in short, to lay all upon the altar, and then to believe, upon the naked testimony of God's word, without any regard to my own feelings, that he accepted it. This seemed the most difficult thing in the world to do. It seemed, indeed, actually impossible. And yet I knew that it was not impossible. I saw that it could and must be done. In this state I remained about two weeks, clearly understanding what I had to do, but not finding how, or not daring to do it.

At length, as I was praying in my room one evening, God's Spirit moved upon me most powerfully then and there to make the required full surrender of myself to him, and believe that I was accepted. My heart shrank back, and I said: "I can not do it." But the Spirit whispered: "It must be done;" and I found myself struggling in the great effort. It was the most solemn hour in all my life. My mind was intensely active. I felt that the interests of three worlds were all centered at one point, and almost before I was aware of it, I was making a full dedication of myself to God, in the strongest manner, and with the most solemn sanctions that I could devise. I wished to enter upon a covenant, that should be in all things "well ordered and sure;"— one that should be irrevocable and eternal. The thought occurred to me that I would put it in writing. I seized my pen for that purpose, but I had not written many words, before a passage of Scripture came to my mind. I turned to 1 Corinthians 1: 30, and read: "For of him are ye in Christ Jesus, who of God is made unto us wisdom, and righteousness, and sanctification, and redemption." I read it with perfect astonishment. "Can it be possible," I exclaimed, "that I have so often read this passage before, and never saw what was in it until now? Why, if Christ is made all this to me, what need I more? Surely, he is all and in all." A flood of light at once broke into my soul. I felt that I had indeed passed over Jordan, and that my soul was in the Canaan of rest. The long conflict was now past, and I realized that for which my soul had so long panted, but which I had scarcely dared hope to enjoy. I could fully trust God to deliver me from all my sins. After some time spent in praising God for his goodness to me, I bethought me of my vow of dedication, which I had begun to write. I had no wish to complete it. So sure did I feel that God had heard and written it in heaven, that it seemed quite unnecessary for me to put it in any poor words of mine.

I felt that God had wrought a great deliverance for me; and so, indeed, he had, as my subsequent experience has abundantly proved. The change which I then experienced was much greater than at my first conversion. The power of sin in me was broken. Particular forms of sin, against which I had struggled all my life, and most frequently in vain, had now lost their hold upon me. The precious promise, "Sin shall not have dominion over you," I could claim, and feel that it was fulfilled within. How I rejoiced in my glorious freedom in Christ. Very many passages of Scripture, which I had never understood before, now seemed clear as day to me. Duties which I had performed with great difficulty, or neglected almost entirely, now became perfectly easy; nay, their performance was a delight. Preaching and pastoral visiting became very different things from what they had ever been before.

Years have now passed since these events occurred, but they are still as fresh in my memory as if it were but yesterday; and although I have often come very far short, and, sometimes *through neglect to testify* to the great work of God in my soul, almost cast away my confidence, and been brought into much difficulty, and many buffetings of Satan, yet I have ever found Jesus faithful to all his promises; and to-day, by his grace alone, I can say that his blood cleanseth from all sin. My confidence in him is stronger than ever. My vows are all renewed, and my sacrifice is lying upon the altar, by the grace of God, never to be removed.

EXPERIENCE OF MISS ———,

A TEACHER IN A BROOKLYN MISSION.

THE consecrated life to which God has called me takes in all *used* and *unused* powers. My pen I have given to Jesus, and my hand. Oh! that these lines "may be a blessing" to some weary friend, longing for the soft hand of Jesus to be placed on their heart, bidding it to cheer up, as he says, "I have overcome the world."

In early life I gave my heart to God, and joined the church. I lived as many do now; loved to go to church, attended to all my duties—in short, *professed* religion. Years rolled on; my father was taken from me, singing, as he went, the praises of Jesus. Then life, real, earnest life commenced. God has taken many ways to bring this will, this life into subjection to his will. Death took away loved ones, adversity took others. "Every heart knoweth its own bitterness." I need not say more. I need not tell how many were the ways taken by God to bring me where he wanted me to be, through severe discipline; but, looking back upon it all, I can say I would not alter one line of life's history. He knoweth best. "He doeth all things well."

Three years ago, after being a Christian for ten years, I was conscious of a deep hunger of soul—a hunger that no earthly love could satisfy. I was thirsty, and earth's springs were dry. Coming to God, and asking sincerely and *believingly* for the bread whereof if a man eat he will hunger no more, and the water whereof if a man drink he will thirst no more, I heard, coming from the lips of Christ himself: "Come unto me, O weary one; *come to me.*"

> "I came to Jesus as I was,
>   Weary, and worn, and sad;
> I found in him a resting-place,
>   And he has made me glad."

To condense much in a little space, *I took Jesus for what I wanted.* I wanted, first, the consciousness of a clean heart. I waited at the cross, where the blood flows, and, when it had washed me clean, the blessed Holy Spirit moved in and took up his abode;

and now my heart was a home for Jesus. Oh! what condescension in him to come thus to dwell with fallen man!

> "The mountain foxes have their hole,
> The sky-birds have their nest;
> But, save in thy surrendered soul,
> HE has not where to rest."

So I bid the "Man of sorrows" welcome. I took Jesus for *purity*, for *rest*, for *love*, and he took me for his own. He appeared to me and said: "Yea, I have loved thee with an everlasting love; therefore with loving-kindness have I drawn thee." Three blessed years have passed—years of usefulness and happiness; for "holiness, usefulness, and happiness are inseparable." Life is real, full of meaning; but life is blessed when given to God, for he gives eternal life back. Oh! who will be so foolish as to miss this holy life? May none who read this be mistaken in God's will. "Be ye holy."

My life-work is teaching school—"teaching school for Jesus," I like to say; teaching poor children. It is blessed work; the giver gets so much more than she gives. Work is good; work makes me hungry, and, coming to Him, I get fed; work makes me tired, and, coming to God, I get rested. I feel the sublimity of service; glad to do some little thing for struggling humanity. Was not this our Saviour's life-work, to help somebody? "Follow thou me." I desire to do so. Oh! for the "mind that was in Christ." "Occupy till I come." When he calls, may we answer, and in the service on high dwell forever with him who died to secure heaven for us.

EXPERIENCE OF C. W.

MY first religious impressions were received when quite young, by reading in a little story-book the account of a Sunday scholar, who had learned to love the Lord Jesus Christ. She was a very sickly child, and used often to repeat those beautiful lines:

> " Jesus can make a dying bed
> Feel soft as downy pillows are."

Being, like her, a very delicate child, subject to severe fits of sickness, the narrative affected me deeply. Many times I wished to know how to pray, for I supposed I should die very young; and oh, what a dreadful fear of death I had! But it pleased the Lord to spare my life, and permit me to grow up to womanhood, amid circumstances which tended to stifle all these early desires to be saved. I was taken into the world for enjoyment, and began to imagine that I was enjoying myself. And why not, when I could go to just as many balls and parties as I wished? And yet there were many drawbacks to my pleasures; for after a night of wordly enjoyment, I was almost invariably sick the next day, and conscience would upbraid me, so that all my peace was gone. At length everything seemed hollow and empty to me — there was nothing real and substantial. I was sick at heart, while my companions seemed to be enjoying themselves. I could not then understand it; but I now see that it was the Spirit of God striving with me—for no living being had ever spoken to me on the subject of religion, and I very seldom went to church.

Just toward the close of one winter season, I made an engagement to go to a ball, after attending many others; but, immediately, I was so harrassed about it that it seemed to me I would go beside myself. I thought if God would only make a way for me to get clear of the engagement, I would serve him forever. On the day of the ball I went to my room, and there, for the first time in my life, knelt in prayer to God, that he would keep me from doing anything of that kind again. I felt that something would hinder me; I did not know nor care, so long as I could be kept from sinning in that way again. Strange as it may appear, as I was coming down-stairs from my room, a person came from the gentleman who had given me the invitation, with a message to me. Without any ceremony or apology, I sent word to him that I was not going. Unladylike as this may seem to the world, I was truly thankful for the release.

I then began trying to fulfil what I had, in my blindness and ignorance, promised God. But oh, how soon I found I could not live one hour without sinning. And even if I could, what was to become of all those sins I had committed from my youth? I tried to read the Bible, but that condemned me more and more. I knew not what to do. If I tried to pray, my sins would rise mountain high, and there was no one I could tell my feelings to. I felt that "no man cared for my soul." I wondered why it was so, and yet I knew I deserved to be cast off, and felt that God would be just in sending my soul to hell. But oh, the awful thought of being cast off forever! I tried to find something on which I could rest, but it was all in vain.

One day, while I was in this state of mind, an acquaintance called to ask respecting the state of mind of a member of our family who was very sick at the time. Instead of answering her inquiries, I commenced weeping for myself, and told her how wretched I was. Her sympathies were enlisted at once, and she asked me to go to church with her. I went, but found no comfort. This was the latter part of July, 1846, and so I went on until the 15th of September, when I listened to a funeral sermon from these words: "The last enemy that shall be destroyed, is death." It was truly awful to me, and I feared that reason would be dethroned. On the next day my pastor sent me the tract entitled: "What is it to believe on Jesus Christ?" I took it to my room and read it, and prayed that the Lord would show me what it was to believe on him aright. My agony was intense. I had scarcely broken my fast for two days, and I could not sleep. That night I resolved, if the Lord would spare my life until the next morning, I would go and see the pastor. It was a dull, murky morning; but at ten o'clock I started for my friend to accompany me. She was anticipating the visit, and was all ready.

On arriving at the pastor's residence he received us very kindly, and, after some words of encouragement, he pointed me so tenderly to Christ, and then knelt and prayed so fervently for me, that I began to feel as if the Lord had heard his petitions, and I said: "I don't believe it is so hard to trust him, after all." He replied: "No; only give yourself right up to him now, for he has loved you with an everlasting love, and he will save you."

I started to go home, but stopped at my friend's house to wash my face; for I had been weeping very much, and my eyes were red and swollen. I asked for some water, and in a moment my friend brought some in a bowl and placed it on a low chair, so low, that I could not reach it without kneeling. In an instant I knelt, and at once there went up from my heart the earnest prayer: "Lord, wash me in thine own blood, as I now wash my face with water." Language fails to tell what I knew and felt at that happy moment. I was washed from my sins—I was saved. I know not how long I knelt there, but when I rose to my feet, I felt as if I was in another world. Everything was changed. The sun had broken forth in full splendor—the streets looked bright —an old hydrant that was near our house had been broken for a long time, and I had often listened to the water running from it, but it never sounded so sweetly before; for I felt that just as freely as that water ran, so freely Christ's blood was poured out for me.

On entering the house, the first thing I did was to open my Bible. It was a new book; every word was full of comfort and consolation. A friend, on seeing the change, said:—" This will not always last; you will have dark hours—every one has them," but

> " I could not believe
> I ever should grieve,
> I ever should suffer again."

On the first Sunday in November, 1844, I was buried with Christ in baptism and united with the Berean Baptist church, N. Y. For some time I was very happy, but I soon found out the truth of my friend's advice. Trials and temptations came, and I yielded to unbelief, and became subject to most terrible fits of despondency. At times my faith would be more strong, and my love to Christ more ardent, and then how delightful my experience would be! But it would not last. This way of "sinning and repenting" seemed so ridiculous to me at times, and yet I could find no other way. If any mortal felt thankful that the fountain stood open all day, I think it was me. I used to think if the Lord would only use me as the instrument of converting one soul, I should be sure that I was accepted. At length he was pleased to use me for the conversion of more than one. But Satan suggested that Judas fulfilled his mission, and so I was troubled still. Oh, how I longed to be free from sin. The more I tried, the worse I got.

About this time the pastor of a neighboring church began to preach on the higher Christian life, or entire consecration to God. The doctrine was opposed by some of the members of his church, and in consequence of this he resigned and organized a new church where he might preach this doctrine without opposition. One of the members of the old church, in whom I had been particularly interested, told me about the matter in a way that prejudiced my mind very much. She said that he professed *sinless perfection*. I replied, "Is there no one we can trust? I always believed him honest and sound; but if that is his doctrine I do n't want any more to do with him." Instantly something seemed to say to me: "What right have you to condemn what you know nothing about?" I was cut to the heart, and would gladly have taken back what I had said. I had frequently heard him preach, but not since he had been brought into this new experience. I therefore determined to go and hear for myself. I went, and I must say I never heard him or any one else preach such sermons before. There was so much of Jesus in them. My heart was melted. I saw he had what I wanted: a living faith in a complete and present Saviour. He did not need to wait to be dead in order to be saved—he was saved already. So far from thinking himself perfect, he constantly affirmed his own nothingness, but held up Christ as all-sufficient.

I had from the first believed that my Lord was able and willing to give me more than I then enjoyed, but I did not know how to secure it. My sins would constantly rise up between my Saviour and myself, and I could not overcome them. I did not doubt but that I should be finally saved from falling into sins and doubts here, so that I might live to the glory of God, and be more useful in his service.

In the spring of 1862 I went to one of the sanctification meetings, held in the Antioch Church, and there heard a brother relate his experience of sanctification. Oh, how ashamed I felt when I looked at him; so much younger than myself, and yet how much more he knew about Jesus and his power to save from sin than I did. I seemed to be starving in the midst of plenty; but I there resolved, God helping me, to know more of Christ as a Saviour. I determined at once to consecrate my all to him. But what had I, a poor worm of the dust, to give? I thought I would just give my poor self, with all I had, to Jesus, to be wholly and forever his. I had no sooner made the attempt, than my only surviving parent, dearer to me than life, rose before me, and the tempter said: "If you consecrate him to the Lord, he will be taken away from you, and what then will you do? You cannot make a living—you cannot do without him." I always felt he was all the world to me; but I never knew how much I did love him, till then. He seemed doubly dear to me; yet the Holy Spirit enabled me to bring him to the altar of consecration, and give him up to Jesus. I felt that if he stripped me of everything—father and all—if he would only give me himself as my Saviour from sin, I should have all I needed.

Jesus accepted my poor offering, and gave me himself, and oh, what a gift! The more I know him the more insignificant I find myself to be. And yet I know he loves me and fully saves me. He has since then taken my dear father from me by death, but I have Jesus, and what can I want more?

EXPERIENCE OF R. A. S.

IN the village of Pawlings, Dutchess Co., N. Y., in the winter of 1866 and 1867, I was first awakened to a sense of my need of a Saviour. I could see the road I was travelling, and had been travelling for years, and knew that the end of that road was approaching, which is everlasting torment. Oh, how I groaned in my soul, when I thought of the friends who are in the world of glory. I thought of seeing them in the general judgment, crowned with glory, and rejoicing with exceeding great joy, while I was trembling before my God, as a conscious sinner, awaiting my awful doom. Oh, how I strove to drive off these feelings! But it was all in vain. They would occupy and harass my mind, and I could not rest, until I found rest in believing on the glorious Son of God. But this for a time seemed an impossible act for me. I would say: "I do believe in Jesus Christ. I believe he is my

Saviour;" but still I could not feel it to be so. Sometimes I thought I could not be saved, because it was too late; I had been too vile. But certain passages of Scripture came to my mind: "He that cometh unto me I will in no wise cast out." "The Son of Man is come to seek and to save that which was lost." "The blood of Jesus Christ, his Son, cleanseth us from all sin." Still it seemed very difficult, yes, impossible to believe, till the following words came to my ears: "Do you believe that Christ is the Saviour? Do you believe that Christ's blood saves you? Do you believe he is willing to save you? Do you believe he will do what he has promised?" I could answer all these questions in the affirmative, but the question came next, placing Christ's saving act in the present tense: "Do you believe that he saves you now? Do you believe *you are saved?*" These two questions remained unanswered for a time. But one evening, at a protracted meeting in the Baptist church, under a sermon preached from Mark 1: 24, I was greatly troubled, and resolved to do all I could to gain Christ. But all I could do was of no avail.

One evening, soon after the above, I heard another sermon from Luke 10: 42: "Mary hath chosen that good part." After preaching, all were requested to make it known, if "they had chosen that good part." I felt something in my heart saying, "You have chosen that good part," and from that night I felt my load of sin gone. Then I could say, I know that Jesus saves me now; blessed be the Lord. I am a sinner "saved by grace," through simple faith on the Son of God. That night I lost all my inclination for the once enjoyed and esteemed games—such as cards, dominoes, dice, etc. Besides, I must confess, I had given my body for a liquor-vessel. Here came the cross: I must no more enjoy a game of euchre; I must bid an everlasting farewell to the bar-room; but I had a Friend in need, and by his help I am what I am. "Old things have passed away, and all things are new;" new and delightful.

In February, 1867, I united with the Baptist Church, and, in April of the same year, I left for the West. I now became greatly troubled, and could not rest with the hope I had. I wanted to be "perfectly conformed to the will of God," and I knew there were higher stages in the divine life which I needed to attain. Jesus says:

"Blessed are the pure in heart, for they shall see God." Paul says, that the end of the commandment is "love out of a pure heart." Oh! how I sighed, and prayed that I might be purified from all sin! I felt there were still some "roots of bitterness" that should be destroyed, or they would again spring up, and trouble me. I wanted to be freed from these remains of the carnal mind; so I determined to purge myself, by God's help, from all worldly and sinful things. I struggled day and night, but with no success, till one evening after reading some tracts treating on entire consecration and holiness, and feeling very sad and miserable, I went to my bedroom, knelt down and prayed, striving with God in prayer, but no victory came to my soul. I felt that there was something yet to be done, but what I knew not. At this point, I was struck with the suggestion evidently of the Spirit, "Cast thy burden upon the Lord." I said: "Here, Lord, I am a burden to myself, take me and do with me as thou seest fit." But all was yet dark, and in this state I retired to my bed, overcome with sorrow. But, blessed be the Lord, I had not been in bed long, when such glory burst in upon my soul, and the room in which I lay appeared as if it were lighted with the glory of God. Oh, blessed be the Lord, my poor soul was filled, and it could hold no more, and I laid and shouted: "O my God, I have seen thy glory, and my soul is free." And I heard a voice in my soul, saying: "This is the sanctifying presence of the Holy Spirit." My very soul seemed filled with glory. I longed to be free from this world that I might forever enjoy this glory! I felt as if I was wrapped up in the mantle of God's love, and very near the heavenly world. Oh, how I love the Lord, for he has done great things for my soul! Oh, how shall I express the joy that is in me? I have been redeemed, and am consciously saved in Christ Jesus. My soul now goes out after those who are not freed from the bondage of sin. Christ purchased a full salvation for you. He has accomplished it in me and will in every one, if you will but come aright—that is, in humility and simplicity. Oh, come all, and taste of the good things of Christ.

EXPERIENCE OF MRS. A. S.

VERY early in life I was the subject of religious impressions. There was a female prayer-meeting at our house, during which I felt that I was a great sinner, and exposed to hell. I asked my mother if she thought the Lord would ever forgive my sins. She answered, "Yes, if you feel what you say when you ask him." "I do," said I. In the agony of my soul I offered in secret the publican's prayer, "God be merciful to me, a sinner." My fear of going to hell was so great, that one day when I was left alone I knelt down beside my little chair and asked the Lord to forgive all my sins; when I arose my burden was gone. The Bible looked good to me; and when in school I read in my Testament the words, *God*, *Lord*, *Jesus*, &c., they seemed very precious and sweet to me. I felt that my sins were all forgiven, and was very happy. I loved the people of God, especially those who lived nearest to him.

One summer my school-teacher, who was, as I thought, a true Christian, often went at noon into a grove to pray. I chose to go with her, while my mates were at play, and there kneel with her while she offered prayer. I delighted much in the Sabbath-school and other religious exercises, and for quite a length of time lived in the sunlight of Jesus' love. By-and-by came doubts and fears, but I prayed the Lord to show me if I was not a Christian, that I might not be deceived, nor deceive others. I feared I might be a hypocrite. Thus I lived year after year, mourning over my sins and forming new resolutions only to prove their weakness. The Lord came and removed my mother by death. In my affliction I clung closer to my Saviour for help, and became less attached to the world. I saw I had been too worldly-minded, but now earthly things looked quite insignificant. I tried to watch and pray more, and live nearer to Jesus; yet often I would say,

> " 'Tis a point I long to know,
> Oft it causes anxious thought:
> Do I love the Lord or no;
> Am I his, or am I not?"

In about a year after the death of my mother I was married, and, as we had but little to commence with, I soon became anxious to secure a home of our own; for this I worked very hard and gave away very little for benevolent purposes. I had so much to do that sometimes I neglected secret prayer and the reading of the word of God. We had family prayer; but I am ashamed to say my mind was so much engrossed with work that I enjoyed it but little. Still I loved the duties of religion, and did not wholly neglect them for the world. I often accused myself of worldliness, and would almost give up my hope, yet I knew I loved the brethren and the cause of Christ. I lived thus for some time, until God came and took away one of my children, and opened my eyes to my true condition. The winter before this event I was enjoying myself well, as I thought, in religion, and in our worldly affairs. We were now for the first time living alone, and I was happy in the society of my two little ones. I read and prayed with them, although they were not old enough to understand much; but I felt that I could not commence too early to guide their young minds in the way of the Lord. Very often when praying I felt that my heart was not right. I asked the Lord to strip me of everything that hindered me from finding an access to the throne of grace, and that I might be just what he would have me to be. I was deeply impressed with the thought that the Lord was preparing a trial for me. What it was I could not tell. "It is possible I think too much of my children," thought I. "Were they my idols?" In June the Lord came and took one, and then in January the other. When I saw that the last one was gone, I felt that I was such a sinner that God had come out in judgment against me, and thus expressed myself to a sister, while standing by her dying couch. "Whom the Lord *loveth* he chasteneth," was the answer. These words comforted me much. I felt it was all just and right, and what I knew not now I should know hereafter. I believed it to be all for my spiritual good. "He doeth all things well." I felt my dependence more and more, and the necessity of living nearer to Jesus, while my love for him grew stronger, and in faith I could say: "I *know* that all things work together for good to them that love God."

In the spring of 1856 our pastor preached much on self-examination, and I became anxious to know of a certainty whether I was a child of God or not. One Sabbath, after meeting, being in great agony of soul, I walked the house, silently praying, "Oh, that I knew my sins were all forgiven." I had desired for years that I might feel willing to die while in health, that I might thereby be sure I was a child of God. That night I dreamed that the Lord was gathering his people together. I thought I stood near a company that was separated from the world's people, and I said to myself: "Now I am going; I am surely one of his; he will take me." But, alas! something was wanting in my dress; it was not all complete. I must get something more for a covering for my shoulders; I was greatly distressed, and in my sorrow I awoke. I thought myself like the five foolish virgins that took no oil with them. But while I was meditating and asking the Lord what this could mean, he showed me that it was a lack of FAITH; that I must BELIEVE more fully in him. Then my prayer was: "Lord, help me to believe; I cannot, unless thou dost help me." I felt he could help me to believe. I saw I must give up ALL —my husband, my children, and all—and submit entirely to his will, should he see fit to take them.

During the following summer, in calling upon

Jesus, I felt great peace of mind; was much enlightened by "Pilgrim's Progress." While on my knees in prayer, I was enabled to give up my family to the Lord, and thank him for afflictions. My eyes were opened, and I saw how just and merciful he was, and felt to praise him for what he had done for me. I did not say much about this experience, listening to the temptation: "What will they say of you, if you thank the Lord for afflictions." Thus, after a while I was justly deprived of my assurance, and became anxious about myself again. I said to myself: "I wish I could be so sick that I should not expect to get well, to see if I would be willing to die." It is a mercy the Lord did not leave one so full of unbelief.

In a few weeks I was taken very ill; my friends thought I would die. When I was first taken ill I said to a friend: "It is a fearful thing to fall into the hands of the living God;" and truly did I feel that it was. He had taken me at my word. For two weeks I knew not what passed. But Jesus was merciful, and in looking to him I was saved. And I could say: "To depart and be with Christ is far better than to live." I cannot express the joy and peace that now filled my soul. The world and friends were out of my mind—Jesus alone filled every thought. I felt my sins were all forgiven, and I had *perfect love* in my soul. Such love for everything God had made, even the merest insect, as I never felt before. I thought this was like a *second conversion*. I felt I never should go astray again. My heart overflowed with thankfulness to God for everything. My doubts and fears were all gone; and, though seven years have passed, they have never returned.

But the Lord was to prove the grace he had given. In 1857 we were a happy family. The Lord had given us two more children, and we enjoyed them much. One day as I was alone it appeared to me that my little girls were not to stay with us long. Dreadful thought! I sat down and took my Bible to find something to comfort me, as I was wont to do while in trouble, and prayed the Lord to help me to be reconciled to his will. I felt that whatever the Lord saw fit to do would be right. In less than a month the Lord came and took the oldest, after three days' illness. I think I felt submission to his will. But my love clung closer to the other; in less than a week she died also. I felt that I should sink beneath the rod.

In the hour of struggle I cried, "O Lord, help me; keep me from sinning against thee." In a few moments I gave her up, saying, "The Lord doeth all things well; though he slay me, yet will I trust in him." He sweetly sustained me through all my afflictions and trials, and I have fully proved the truth of the promise: "My grace is sufficient for thee."

The Lord had yet to prove my willingness to obey. He showed me that it was my duty to go and talk with an ungodly neighbor, who seldom heard the gospel preached, about his soul. I was enabled to obey, and was much blessed. I regret, however, that I have not *always* as readily obeyed the voice of the Spirit. I had never offered prayer in public, but during a protracted meeting I saw that I must do that duty. I saw that I had neglected it through pride for fear my prayers would not sound well to others; but now my eyes were opened, and, after a struggle with the enemy, Jesus gave me the victory, and since then it has been more a privilege than a cross. The Lord has blessed me much since I gave up my will entirely in every matter to him; but how much have I lost by not taking up this cross when I first started in the way of truth!

I lay myself in Jesus' arms, willing to live or die—willing he should do with me and mine just as he sees fit. Now I can give more to the work of the Lord "without grudging," trusting him for all things. I praise the Lord that he has not left me, so stubborn, to myself. It is a merciful Jesus alone that has saved me.

EXPERIENCE OF A STRUGGLING PASTOR.

NEARLY twenty years ago I was passing from "The Hill" at Hamilton to the boarding-hall, when a dear brother, now many years in heaven, passed his arm affectionately through mine, and inquired of my spiritual welfare and progress.

After a short conversation, he placed in my hands a little book, "Mahan on Christian Perfection," with the request that I would carefully and prayerfully read it. I did as requested, and, before its perusal was finished, became profoundly convinced that whether the philosophy of the writer was correct, and his choice of terms judicious or not, one thing was sure: there was attainable for the Christian a "higher life," a deeper experience than had yet been mine.

I saw very clearly that I was not entirely consecrated to God, was not wholly set apart to his service, and that my will was by no means lost in his. I saw, too, not only the reasonableness of God's claim upon me for entire consecration, but that such consecration or sanctification was not more a reasonable duty than a *promised Gospel blessing*. I came at once "under conviction." And now, as I write, I feel a strong desire to pass over about eighteen years of my life, with the simple remark that I remained "under conviction" all that time. But the thought that possibly some brother or sister may be benefited thereby, impels me to the relation of a few recollections of my life and experience during that time.

It was a matter of course, perhaps, that one of the first questions arising in my mind should be, "How shall I attain this blessed state?" In seeking the answer to this question, I inquired, "How have others attained it?" and read almost everything in the way of religious biography, and of books professing to guide those seeking a closer walk with God, within my reach. I read the Bible, too, carefully and prayerfully.

Perhaps I gained all the light that I was prepared to follow and improve; but it seems to me now, that some of the impressions made upon my mind were a hindrance rather than a help to me. Thus I came early to think that most, if not all, who had ever attained this state, had been more than ordinarily faithful and devoted Christians before such attainment, and had been very earnest and persevering in seeking it. This idea, associated as it was in my mind with a sense of my own weakness and unfaithfulness, was, at times, a source of great discouragement. Others, it seemed to me, might be faithful and successful seekers for this blessing; but as for me, when I resolved ever so strongly to pray, and watch, and deny myself, my prayers would soon become formal, and then be neglected; my watchfulness would cease before I knew it, and my self-denial become a wearisome burden to me.

Oh! a hundred times, I suppose, I have looked back over my pathway, all strewn, as it was, with broken resolutions, shattered hopes, and withered aspirations, and felt, with a deep heart-sickness that I cannot express, that I could not be faithful—that I was the captive, the bond slave of my carnal weakness and depravity. Often would the thought come over me: this very blessing which others have faithfully sought and found, I need to make me faithful. I now know this to be true, and I *think* it was a suggestion of the Holy Spirit, a whisper of the voice behind me, saying: "This is the way, walk ye in it."

There was another obstacle in my way. I could not earnestly and hopefully seek this blessing, because I was almost always conscious of an unwillingness to yield my will in everything, my purposes, plans, hopes, and indulgences, all up to God. This unwillingness destroyed, of course, all my confidence in prayer. How could I pray for the Holy Spirit, when I knew that I was unwilling to be led by him? How could I pray to be sanctified wholly, to be made a living sacrifice, when I was conscious that my heart recoiled from the altar?

There were, it is true, times, many times, seasons of revival, scattered along through those years, when I seemed, for a time, to give up all *for* God and *to* him. But if, for a little time, I dreamed that my will was lost, I would very soon find my mistake corrected. Some test act or question would be brought before me, and I would discover that "the law in my members" was still a living power, and I a captive still.

In the fall of 1856, I think it was, this question of submission to God's will came up very distinctly before my mind. I had been for some time more than usually revived in my religious emotions—had been praying and laboring with more than usual zeal, but had been much assailed by temptation and often overcome. I was wearied somewhat with the struggle, when one day, while sitting in my study, the whole subject of entire consecration to God seemed to come up before me. The question seemed to come up for decision *then:* "Was I willing to give up all, and take Jesus for my master in *everything;* to be guided in every act and wish of my life by him?"

My poor rebellious heart drew back. I was not willing. In a moment my mind was dark, all dark. I fell on my knees, but I could not pray. Every word died ere it came to my lips. I could only say, "God be merciful to me a sinner."

Months, years rolled away, before that cloud was once lifted from my spirit. My heart ached very often in view of the decision I had made, and yet I seemed to have no power to reverse it. Still, I continued steadily preaching, and going the round of my pastoral duties. To many, this will seem a marvel; but I dared not stop. A necessity seemed laid upon me, and a woe if I did not preach the Gospel.

At times, I was terribly tempted to disbelieve the Gospel, and the reality of experimental religion; never, however, very long at a time. When

I looked out on the dark, cheerless, shoreless ocean of infidelity, my soul recoiled. I said I had rather cling to the Bible and be deceived, if I must, than be afloat on that ocean. I think so still. But now I have no thought of being deceived. I know in whom I have believed.

The winter and spring of 1857-'8, all remember as a time of peculiar religious awakening. Very many remember it as a time of peculiar blessing to themselves. It was to me as the year of jubilee. During the fall and winter, God's Spirit was very graciously poured out upon our community. I felt the power of the revival, and rejoiced in it. I do not, however, remember having any special exercises with reference to my own state, until about the first of February. Indeed, I felt that the cloud of which I have spoken was still upon me, and I doubted much if it would ever pass away. Still, in looking back upon those days, I think I can see that I was becoming more truly and deeply humbled, and more ready to give up my will to God than ever before.

In January, 1858, some rather severe trials came across my path—trials which tested to some extent my willingness to say, "Thy will be done." I believe, that, more fully than at former times,

I was enabled to say it, and to choose God's will as mine.

Early in February, I do not remember the day, nor any attending events, but I well remember the fact, I seemed to wake up as from a dream. A new sensation, one I had never felt before, seemed to fill me, to permeate my whole being. It was not excited feeling, it was not joy. It was peace—deep, calm, perfect peace. It was love, unutterable love. It was light, an atmosphere of light, in which my soul seemed bathed, and which seemed to penetrate body and soul alike.

One of the first mental exercises which I recollect was, that the inquiry seemed flashed across my mind, "Are you *now willing* that God should be your master in everything? Will you take his will as yours without the least reserve? Are you quite willing that he shall appoint you crosses and afflictions, and blast your worldly hopes and joys, if he sees best?" My thought was, "I will examine myself; I will not answer hastily." But immediately the reply seemed to come welling up from the depths of my heart: "Oh, not *willing!* That is not quite the word; *but glad!* oh, *so glad!* that he will be my master!" How could I ever have hesitated, even for a moment, to choose his will for mine? How could I so distrust his love and wisdom? All the fears I had had of trials and crosses he might send me were gone, utterly gone. I could realize now that "perfect love casteth out fear."

"And this," says my brother, "you call, I suppose, second conversion, or sanctification. I do not see that there is anything peculiar in it, so different from what most of us experience many times in the course of our lives. It was, indeed, a very pleasant revival of religious sensibility. I do not see in it more than this."

Well, to me it is a *new experience*—different, certainly different from anything in my former life. I am not anxious as to what it shall be called, or whether it be named at all. I only care to tell, as plainly as I can, what God has done for my soul. I would bear a testimony for him. I feel a debt of love to Jesus resting upon me, which eternity will not be long enough for me to pay. I would, at least, publicly acknowledge the debt. Then, too, I know that there are many of my brothers and sisters, who are now groaning under the yoke of bondage, which was long upon my neck. I would tell them of my deliverance, "that the law (power) of the Spirit of life in Christ Jesus hath made me free from the law (power) of sin and death."

But they will ask, perhaps, "Does your experience remain what it was at first?" I reply, no, and yes. I have not at all times felt during the months and years that have passed, I do not now feel, all the gushing sweetness and tenderness of the first few days. But I do feel that I am as fully consecrated to Christ; that my whole spirit, and soul, and body, are presented a "living sacrifice" to him, as fully as then. I believe that I do not love him less, or trust him less than then.

Now I know that to some of the dear people of God, it will be very likely to seem that this frank expression of my thoughts is an unpleasant exhibition of self-confidence, or spiritual pride. And I know that it would, probably, be in vain for me to try to remove that impression. I shall not try. I will only remark, that if I am not proud, it is only because he who has *promised to keep me* does as he has *promised to do.*

EXPERIENCE OF O. A.,

A NORWEGIAN SAILOR.

I WAS born in the northern part of Europe. My religious creed was the dead formula of the Lutheran church, without power. I well remember, at times, when reading in our church books of the new birth, that I used to wonder what it meant, and often purposed to live a strict moral life, but of course failed of attaining any knowledge of God's grace.

In the year 1833 I came to this country as a common seaman before the mast, and two years after became the officer of a vessel. On my first visit to America I thought it was a wicked country, because there were not so many holidays, such as Christmas, Easter, Ascension Day, Midsummer Day, Good Friday, etc., to spend partly in church forms and partly in getting drunk and in sinful frolics.

It pleased the Lord, in 1836, to open my eyes to see my lost condition as a sinner; and then I found all my former religious schemes vain, and, to use a sailor's expression, I threw them all overboard, and took the Bible alone for my guide. I did not know what denominations were, and therefore could not choose any. My teaching I took from the Bible alone, and hence I desired to be baptized as Jesus was, whom I then took to be my leader in all my ways. But I knew not where the people were to be found who did baptize; only I had heard, when a boy, that in England and America there were some of this faith and practice. Through the advice of a minister whose preaching I then attended, I joined a Methodist class. I was very happy for two or three years, and even the motions of sin which were by the law seemed to be suspended, for I felt them not, and I knew I was a new creature in Christ Jesus.

I heard in class meetings and from other sources of sanctification, and prayed earnestly for it, but had no definite idea of what it was. I expected to realize some great inward joyous emotion, or some blessing poured down on the soul, which of itself would impart all things needed, independent of any exercise of faith, or of any personal consecration on my part; and thus I sought in vain.

At length I got married, and in 1840 I and my wife were baptized by Rev. W. W. Everts, and joined the Tabernacle Baptist Church in Mulberry st., N. Y. Soon after this the cares of the world, together with crosses and losses, drew me away from God; and being now associated with those who did not believe in the experience of sanctification until death, I began to entertain the same idea, that I never could be freed from the power of sin in this life. I looked at Scripture marks and standards, and prayed for grace, and confessed my backslidings, until I was ashamed of my own prayers, and often said, in covenant meetings, that I was not satisfied with my experience.

In June, 1859, I heard that the pastor of a certain Baptist Church in New York, whom I thought very much of, had resigned, on account of some members of the church opposing his views of sanctification, and that he had organized another church, and took another place of worship. I attended a number of times in their new place of worship, and heard his views in full; and I found them to be clear and Scriptural. In the fall I attended a union meeting in this church, and heard ministers and others connected with, I think, four different denominations, relate their experience of sanctification. I went away in deep contemplation, and, having time at command, I searched the

Bible, and prayed with renewed earnestness, and endeavored to consecrate myself to God; but I dared not believe that I was accepted through Christ, and hence I failed to receive the blessing.

In the latter part of April I went to a meeting in another place, and again heard the same experience from persons of different denominations. On the first day of May I went, with deep emotions, to the same place again, praying all the way that I might come to a decision on this subject. A sister told the first exercises of her mind, and the steps she took to obtain the blessing. She related precisely what had passed in my own soul in secret before God—except that she had claimed the promises and I had not. The great difficulty with her had been to believe that she was accepted on the bare promise without feeling it first, and this difficulty now stood in my way. I knew I had given myself and all I had to God for time and eternity; but how could I believe the promise of entire acceptance fulfilled in me, with nothing to rest on but his naked word? But now, in the name of Jesus, I ventured on him, and said in my soul: "As sure as the immutable God exists, it must be so; I must be accepted; I will believe, come life or death."

From that time I realized a consciousness of sanctification, but scarce dare to admit it even in my own mind. For three or four days after this I experienced the most keen temptations to unbelief I had ever known. The enemy suggested: "What are you more to-day than you were yesterday? What have you more now than before?" For I had no sensible or emotional evidence. A dear disciple had exhorted me to hold on and not go back, and now the enemy said: "What are you resting on—the wind?" "No," said the Spirit, "you are resting on the immutable word of God." One day the enemy tempted me to lay aside all this empty and unwarranted faith I had presumed myself into, as he expressed it, and the Spirit most kindly said: "You have taken a great and important step, and no wonder if Satan should assault your faith with his fiery darts." I said in my heart: "If I must shut my eyes and stop my ears, and cry 'Eternal life,' and if I am assailed with all the malice of hell, yet will I believe on the strength of God's word." At every opportunity I kneeled before God and asked for an evidence of my entire sanctification, and thanked him for such signal deliverance from Satan.

But no sensible evidence came; only a calm consciousness of not having yielded to the enemy. Then came the question with power: "Where is your love to God and man and holiness?" This inquiry went into my soul, and I dared not assert before God that I realized this supreme love. Then I asked myself the question: "Do I hate sin, and all appearance of sin?" Here my whole soul and every faculty in me seemed to start up and answer: "I do hate it with a perfect hatred." By this time the next meeting came on the subject of holiness, and there I related my experience as far as it went. I told of my trials of faith and love, and how the Lord had saved me from yielding; but I dared not say that the Lord had fully saved me. Here a Congregational minister looked me in the face and said: "You have got to come to that." This idea seemed very bold at first, but immediately the thought came: "Yes, sure enough, I have got to come to that. God requires an appropriating faith." I was then enabled to believe that God fully saved me, and have so believed ever since.

Two days after this I awoke in the morning with a sweet heavenly peace in my soul and rest in the

Holy Ghost never before realized by me, and as clear an evidence as I could desire. I realized, as I never had done before, that Jesus then and there saved me from all sin; and, as there was nothing to condemn me but the law, and Christ had redeemed me from under its curse, I was free indeed.

And now I walk by faith; and though I shall never be free from natural imperfections as long as I am in this body, yet I do realize most positively that, as these natural frailties flow out from me every moment, so Jesus, in his priestly office, cleanses them, and atones for them, and I am permitted to know that he is my righteousness and sanctification and redemption so long as I continue in him as the branch abideth in the vine.

> "There is a fountain filled with blood,
>   Drawn from Immanuel's veins;
> And sinners, plunged beneath that flood,
>   Lose all their guilty stains."

EXPERIENCE OF MISS J. F. T.

I SCARCELY remember the time when thoughts of death or eternity did not solemnly affect me. Before I knew the worth of the soul, the belief that I was to die often intruded upon my pleasures. At the age of ten, I had the privilege of reading books an older sister brought from Sunday-school; and one that especially affected me was the memoir of a little girl, a year older than myself. A sense of my sinful nature, as I contrasted it with her life, pained me; and I wept, and longed to be like her, so that God could love me.

When I was twelve years of age, I was convicted of sin, and trust that God, for Christ's sake, forgave me. But I was not satisfied, when comparing my love to Jesus with that of the Sunday-school girl, for I could not say he was my "all in all."

My mother spoke to me of the danger of one so young indulging in a false hope. Had an arrow pierced my heart, I could not have felt a greater pain; but she saw no signs, for I turned my head away, and for three days I almost forgot to eat. At first I thought myself a hypocrite, but knew I had not intended that, and prayed for a new heart, believing I had been deceived. Gaining no evidence of God's favor. I began to think I was guilty of the unpardonable sin, and doomed to despair. Then came the thought, What if there is no God? I tried to resist the insinuation, but when I read the passages in the New Testament, once so full of consolation and Jesus, it seemed there was no Jesus after all. These dreadful feelings left me suddenly, and I seemed to love the Saviour better than before. Still I could not say he was my all.

I did not make a public profession at once, and when, a few years later, a sense of duty urged me thus to do, the same dissatisfaction almost prevented me. I told a friend, who was just beginning to preach, of my lack of liberty, and he said all felt just so; "Go right forward, and live it down." I trusted this could be done, and was baptized.

The more I read the Bible, the more I saw it the duty of every Christian to forsake the world entirely, and set an example that should win souls to God. I hit right and left, whenever my sense of Christian consistency was outraged; and when worldly professors told me religion had nothing to do with our worldly affairs, and the reason of my feeling so was because I had not learned the ways of the world, I could answer, that it was hypocrisy, that it was perjury, while professing to be a follower of Jesus, to take *the ways of the world* for our pattern. Then I would pray for them, and weep in secret over my unamiable manners toward my elders, till I had the assurance of Jesus' pardon.

As I grew older, I did learn something of "the ways of the world," and alas! that I should not have been obliged to go outside the church for this knowledge! Imperceptibly, a desire for worldly honors grew up in my heart, and I *tried* to believe that Christians *could* do no better than they did, while in contact with the world; still, from the deepest recess of my heart would occasionally come the reproof, "Ye cannot serve God and mammon."

In the winter of 1852-3, I improved an opportunity to go West, in the family of an acquaintance, as teacher. I found a large society of Christian people, and I certainly believed there must be much devotion. The second year, the pastor came to board with the family where I lived, and I promised myself much benefit from the pious influence of those he would draw around him. But

I was disappointed. I looked within and without. I had flattered myself that the very little I followed after the world was no sin; but as my proud, foolish heart was again lighted up by God's unchanging truth, my whole soul was disgusted, and I felt that if all besides me could serve God and mammon, *I could not.* I was wretched, and gladly did I welcome the time when I could leave the gay town of C. for my native State.

I was now called to part with a beloved nephew. Amiable, generous, just, a scholar, and above all a Christian, I had looked forward to the time when his influence should be brought to bear upon those about him, and confidently hoped the high tone of his character would win them to a holier, purer devotion. But suddenly he was stricken and died. The bitter grief that filled my heart first aroused me to see that I was far from being ready to give up my soul to God. I tried to seek the Lord more diligently, and *did* enjoy more of his presence than ever before; but I was not satisfied.

I went again West the following winter (1857-8), and, to my great annoyance, had to pass most of the time in a family of spiritualists. They were formerly Baptists, the old gentleman a deacon of good repute; his daughters were now what they termed mediums. The father urged me to look into the doctrine. I read his papers and witnessed the performance of the daughters, till I learned what they believed, and all they could do. Then he said, "You see it is not all humbug. You see the state of religion in the churches, and that some change is necessary." "Yes," I replied, "I have long felt this deeply." "Well, spiritualism is just the thing; it is so comforting to know our departed friends are near. My old faith could not have sustained me." He then urged me to give my opinion. I told him I could sooner believe in *no* God, than exchange the gracious influences of the Holy Spirit upon the heart and conscience for clairvoyance and house-hauntings generally; and if there was any thing in it not accounted for in nature, I believed it the work of Satan. He cast upon me a look of pity, and left the room.

The summer and fall of '58 brought me peculiar temporal trials. My earthly trust had nearly *all* been destroyed, and still stern affliction awaited me. The fact that death would soon separate us all from every earthly good, however much we might be favored, chilled the desire therefor. I had battled with the world just as long as I could; for pride and will no longer came to my aid. What should sustain me now? I must have a *faith*, deeper, broader, higher.

In the winter of 1858-59, I felt urged to give up the world and all the affairs of this life into the hands of God. Satan said, "A leap in the dark. *Beware!* who ever trod this way?" True, *I knew* no mortal that had, but I could beware no longer, and bowed helplessly, saying: "Thy will, O God, be done; only save me from my vileness." A peace, deep and abiding, took possession of my soul. All bitter repining and murmuring ceased. I had nothing to complain of, for I felt that God had done all things well. Before I was aware, I was saying to Jesus, "Thou art my *all in all.*" When reading in the Bible of being "dead to the world, and alive to God," my heart would quickly respond; but I checked such thoughts; for who but the apostles dare presume to say that? Two years I tried to keep these feelings down, and gather up something like my old interest in the affairs of earth, but in vain; and I began to believe, more and more, that all Christians should feel just as I did.

About this time a brother sent me a book entitled "The Higher Christian Life." My heart was full of joy, for all was explained. There *were* others that had experienced the same change that I had. Some called it "full salvation," others "sanctification by faith," or "entire sanctification," all meaning the same. I called it *"giving up all for Jesus."*

In February, 1862, during a series of meetings, I felt it would be a great privilege to tell the church of my new-found treasure. Alas! that I should have proved so fearful still—so possessed with *pride*. The fear of being called *fanatic* prevented me. Justly was I deprived of full assurance. I was in this state of mind when a publication reached me which had in it a letter from an acquaintance of mine to the editor, speaking of a change he had experienced, and of his belief in the doctrine of "entire sanctification." I objected to the term strongly, but wrote him, asking his views. In one of his letters to me the truth was made so clear, I felt compelled to find out what my true spiritual condition was. In earnestly seeking to know God's will, it was made clear that I must go to the church, and do the duty I neglected over a year before. At first it seemed a small thing, but the consequences came up, and I felt that I could not do it.

No one can know what I endured in the temptation that followed, only those that have felt in their heart the burning wo of unbelief. For nearly two days I could not believe God would forgive my unwillingness to do his will. In mercy he finally directed me to read Heb. iv., 15, 16. I rested upon the blessed assurance, and again found peace. I felt his grace would be sufficient for me in doing all that he required, still there was no delight in being counted worthy to labor for the blessed Master. I was thinking how many times he had called after me, and of his great forbearance toward one so sinful, when my whole heart went out in gratitude, and I could but exclaim: "O thou blessed Saviour, if in any way thou canst make one like *me* useful in thy cause, here I am; do what seemeth thee good. I have truly deserved thy wrath for refusing so long to obey thee." Something seemed to say: "And you *have his wrath*." The transition from joy in God to a sense of his great anger was instantaneous, and never before could I *think* how AWFUL was the "blackness of darkness" that *could* fill a soul when forsaken of God. The Bible was in my hand, and with an effort I opened it to a passage significant of God's great mercy, and it stayed me up.

A deep calm pervaded my soul. I had not great

joy, but truly the Lord led me beside still waters, where there was nothing to molest or make afraid. In the mean time I was counting the long days that must pass ere the time would come for doing my neglected duty. As the day drew near, how the enemy seemed to throw every obstacle in the way. But, all glory to Jesus, these insinuations found no place in my heart. The appointed time found me in my place. Even here the enemy came with a sweeping assault, as of old; but I felt my heart was all given to Jesus, and I had nothing to say in the matter aside from his interests. For the first time in my life, I arose to speak for God in just the manner he would have me. In no way to encourage pride, I related something of his dealings with my soul.

More than the weight of one year's doubting was removed from my soul. I scarce dare consider how I felt, *so blessed was I.* All glory to Jesus! I have times of temptation and darkness, but *no doubts.* I feel that I *am preserved; kept* by an invisible hand from the power of the foe. Helpless, and unable to do the least thing of myself, yet abundantly blessed in feeling how much I "need," and knowing how much I "have," the merit of Christ's death every moment. "I know that *my*

Redeemer liveth," a *perfect Saviour*, and he in love permits my faith to be tested by temptation, that I may be strengthened and upheld, so as to manifest his praise in all things.

My prejudices are gone. Let all, who *can*, call this wonderful grace other than a sanctifying power; it is all potent to reconcile fully to God, removing every "root of bitterness," and enabling us to "reckon ourselves dead indeed to the world but alive to God through Jesus Christ," in whom we *are preserved* blameless. Praised be the name of the Lord forever, that in his great mercy, through the merits of the blessed Jesus, he has applied its subduing influences, *even* to *my* heart, making me glory in counting myself "less than the least of all saints," the *chiefest* sinner saved by grace.

EXPERIENCE OF C. R.,
ONCE A FASHIONABLE YOUNG LADY.

I WAS born in the city of New York; but, having unconverted parents, I was not religiously educated. I think I never attended Sunday-school more than half-a-dozen times in my childhood, though much that I learned then was retained in my memory, and thought of many a time after I left the school.

When I was about eight years of age, I received a wonderful answer to prayer; and, in fact, I think it was the first prayer I ever offered; for, though I had not been religiously taught, I had an inward consciousness of the existence of a God, and often at midnight I loved to look up into the quiet sky—"that blue abyss of space"—which I felt was inhabited by some great, mysterious Being, and commune, frequently saying:

> "Oh! thou great Being! what thou art
>   Surpasses me to know;
> Yet sure I am, that known to thee
>   Are all things here below."

I felt that God had all power—that he was omnipotent; and I remembered that, on returning from school one day, I made a request of my mother which was not granted, and, on acquainting my Sunday-school teacher with the fact, she told me if we asked anything of God in prayer, he would give it to us. "Now," thought I, "I will go and ask God." I repaired to my room, and, bowing upon my knees, commenced to pray. But I was not satisfied with my kneeling posture; so, casting myself upon the floor, and burying my face in my hands, I continued praying to One whom I now believe bends,

> "'Mid cherubim and seraphim,
> To hear the children's prayer."

I did not rise until I felt that my request would be granted, and an inward assurance was mine that I had "prevailed with God." My request was granted, just as I had expected, and I remember distinctly praising God, and saying: "How easy for God to do anything for us!"

At the age of fifteen I received another answer to prayer. A very precious little pin had been lost, and I was accused of being the guilty or careless one who had been the cause of it. I protested my innocence, but still the pin could not be found. It was rendered doubly dear from having been in the family for many years. I said: "In order to prove to them that I have not lost it, I will ask God that it may be found." And in a most wonderful manner my prayer was answered by a dream, leading me to the very place where it was concealed. Thus, when I was but a child, and a lost sinner, God revealed himself unto me as a God who hears and answers prayer.

The years that followed were spent in the amusements of the world, and I thought I was one of the happiest girls that ever lived—though I must confess there were times when I would become satiated with all these pleasures. My soul longed for something higher and holier. These sensual delights did not fully satisfy, and I remember that frequently, at some evening party, after a dance, I would steal away alone, and in solitude look up into the starry sky, while tears would stream down my face, and I would exclaim: "Oh, what vanity! what vanity! Surely there is something better than this for me!"

One calm summer evening, while visiting a friend in the country, we strolled down the walk and paused beneath the branches of some beautiful trees. The moon shone brightly, and the atmosphere seemed laden with the fragrance of a thousand flowers. We stood silently for some time, when at length the stillness was broken by my friend, speaking as to herself in French, and again repeating in English these words: "Holy, holy art thou, Jesus!" I was awed, for we seemed to be surrounded by a holy presence. I wished that she would repeat the words, and longed to ask her what she knew about Jesus, but did not. The name of Jesus had filled me with strange awe, and, for the first time in my life, I thought all the sounds of nature seemed to be praising the great "First Cause."

At the age of nineteen, having returned to the city of New York, I was converted under the preaching of the Rev. H. Grattan Guinness, the Irish evangelist. It was through the earnest solicitation of a dear schoolmate that I consented to go to church, which I had not done for two whole years.

My decidedly Christian experience began March 27, 1860. Never shall I forget the night I first heard Mr. Guinness preach. The chapter read by him was the 23d of Luke; and his text, the 33d verse of the same chapter: "And when they were come to a place which is called Calvary, there they crucified him." It would be impossible to describe the scene in the sanctuary. Though the house was so crowded that there was scarcely room for another person to stand in the aisles, yet a solemn stillness pervaded the place, and, before the chapter was concluded, I was weeping. *I had never heard it before.* When he commenced to preach, picturing Jesus upon the cross, enduring all the agonies of a most excruciating death, I sobbed aloud; and when he cried: "My God! my God! why hast thou forsaken me?" his face appeared like marble, while tears poured from his eyes, and nearly all in the sanctuary, it seemed to me, were weeping.

This, thought I, is not affectation. No, no; *he believes what he is saying.* It is *all true*—I know it is true. And, oh! how I wished for a Bible, that I might see if all that he had been preaching about was there. But I had not much time for thought, for my mind was upon Calvary and its bleeding victim. I could see the vail of the temple rent in the midst—the fearful darkness that covered the face of the earth when he cried, "It is finished"—the rocks that were rent—the graves that were opened—the dead that came forth. Mingled with these thoughts were feelings of most keen and acute anguish. "For your sins," said the preacher, looking straight at me— "*your sins crucified the Son of God.*" I thought he meant me, and I trembled as he continued: "Yes; your sins, YOUR sins. Jesus so loved YOU, that he was willing to bear YOUR sins in his own body on the tree. He is the Rock cleft for YOU, that in him you might hide, and forever be sheltered from the wrath of an offended God."

He then spoke of the fearful consequences to those who, from that time, dared to reject the Saviour; assuring them that their portion would be a place in the bottomless pit, where the smoke of their torment ascendeth up forever and ever. I was not terrified by this, for my heart was melted with the love of Jesus; and, leaving the sanctuary "silently and prayerfully," as requested by the preacher, I sought the solitude of my room, and, falling on my knees, prayed:

"Oh! Jesus, is it true thou dost love ME? and hast thou loved ME with an everlasting love? Was it MY sins that crucified thee, Jesus?" And then, like a grand panorama, the whole scene passed before me. I could see the mad, delirious throng urging the "Man of Sorrows" on to death, compelling him to bear his cross, as, weary and fainting, he ascended the hill of Calvary and came to Golgotha, "the place of skulls," where many a malefactor had been crucified; and I could hear the dying Saviour, with his last, fainting breath, hoarse with the torments of crucifixion, cry, "It is finished." Before I arose, I solemnly vowed that I would, from that time, know nothing but "Christ crucified."

Early the next morning I bought a little Bible, and, quickly bringing it home, I opened it and read words spoken by the Lord Jesus when he was upon the earth. I cannot tell how sweet they were to me.

The next evening found me again in the sanctuary at an early hour, Bible in hand, intently reading while the crowd was gathering. Oh! it was such a wonderful book! I was struck with its sublimity, and, as I read of the miracles Jesus performed when on the earth—how the lame were made to walk, the deaf to hear, the blind to see, and the dead to live—I exclaimed: "Surely, this was none other than the Son of God!" Thus for weeks I continued to attend the sanctuary, reading my Bible continually, and the Spirit of God was leading me "into all truth."

A short time after this, Mr. Guinness left the city; but I still continued to attend church, and occasionally I would steal away to the prayer-meeting. The change that had taken place in me was so great that it was soon observed by others. I was naturally lively and particularly fond of dress, and now my manner of conversation had become entirely changed. I could not jest or trifle, and every leisure moment was spent in prayer, or the reading of God's Word on my knees. Indeed, so great was my love to the Scriptures that I seemed to more than read—I did eat, yea, greedily devour, "every word that proceeded out of the mouth of God;" and the deeper I searched in this mine of treasure, the more valuable truths were brought to light.

But I soon learned that, if the Bible was true, all the professed Christians I had thus far met were wrong; for, instead of "coming out from the world, and being separate," they were in it so deeply that, by their dress and manners, they could not be distinguished from the world, and instead of loving God with all the heart, soul, strength, and mind, the world had the largest share of their affections; and I further found that, to obey the command, "Be ye holy, for I, the Lord your God, am holy," was considered by them as nothing less than heresy.

But I resolved to pattern after none; and though others were more conformed to the world than I thought the Word of God would warrant, I was taught by the Lord neither to approve nor condemn, but to listen attentively, and obey perfectly, the voice which said: "What is that to thee? follow thou me." This I was determined to do; to follow Jesus in all his requirements, and to die, if need be, for the truth's sake. The world looked to me like a hollow, empty, gaudy bubble. I wondered that everybody could not see it so.

A letter from a kind friend warned me against *enthusiasm*, telling me I must look at the Word in the "sober light of reason, and not through the false medium of enthusiasm;" continuing: "Persons of ardent temperament, like yourself, are prone to take enthusiastic views of everything. Experience and knowledge of the world have, in some measure, corrected my exuberance of sentiment. I know that I am right when I say that enthusiasm will lead into error, even in religious matters; and they err, who, either in dress or conversation, or any other unimportant matters, set themselves against the established customs of those with whom they associate."

This letter had a far different effect from what was intended. It proved most conducive to my spiritual health. I replied firmly, that I could not receive the advice given, as I did not think it consonant with Scripture. The Word clearly taught me that those who have professed Christ are to "be not conformed to this world;" that their conversation was always to be such as "becometh the gospel of Christ;" that they were to be "holy in all manner of conversation;" their dress was not to be that "outward adorning of plaiting the hair, and of wearing of gold, or of putting on of apparel," but "a meek and quiet spirit, which is in the sight of God of great price." Many tried to dissuade me from being so orthodox. Many feared, and said I would soon become a "fanatic." These remarks were from Christians; while unconverted friends (my former associates, from whom I had completely severed myself after inviting them to tread with me the highway of holiness) said I had been *completely spoiled*, and had become "a praying, psalm-singing Methodist."

Up to this time, I had not connected myself with

any church; but I was desirous of identifying myself with the truth, and uniting with the people of God. "But who are the people of God?" I asked myself. Sabbath after Sabbath I went to hear the Gospel preached, but was disappointed; on retiring from the sanctuary, I was forced to exclaim: "They have taken away my Lord, and I know not where they have lain him."

For weeks, I sought direction of God, in earnest prayer. I knew that God, by his Spirit, would lead me to a people who worshipped the true God in spirit and in truth. I believed, and did "not make haste." One Sunday afternoon, while walking up Seventh Avenue, intending to go to church, but I knew not where, I was attracted by the sound of music in a plain-looking house of worship. Ascending the steps, I heard not an organ, nor a choir merely, but many voices, singing in sweet harmony praises to "one Jesus." I had intended to go farther, but "the Spirit suffered me not." I entered, and to my great joy, when the services were ended, I felt that the preacher, with simple and earnest eloquence, had presented "Christ crucified," as the only and all-sufficient Saviour. I went again and again, feeling constrained to acknowledge, every time I came away, "God is with this people, of a truth." I was totally unacquainted with any of the members of the church, but I learned from the pulpit one Sunday the residence of the pastor, and, improving the earliest opportunity, I visited him, and, after relating something of my experience, expressed an earnest desire to unite with the church under his care.

I became daily more and more attached to this people, to whom I knew I had been led by the Spirit of God, until at length I was baptized, and united with them.

My prayer, from the day of my conversion, was, that I might "know Jesus and the power of his resurrection, and the fellowship of his sufferings;" and, being struck with the beautifully-expressive consecration of Madam Guion, I adopted it as my own: "I henceforth take Jesus Christ to be mine. I promise to receive him as a husband to me; and I give myself to him—unworthy though I am—to be his spouse. I ask of him, in this marriage of spirit with spirit, that I may be of the same mind with him—meek, pure, nothing in myself, and united in God's will; and, pledged as I am to be his, I accept as a part of my marriage portion the temptations and sorrows, the crosses and contempt that fell on him."

I thought, when I first began to read the Bible, that the passage, "He that loseth his life for my sake shall keep it unto life eternal," alluded exclusively to those who, like Stephen, suffered martyrdom for the truth; but I soon learned that there was a death, even while we lived, far more excruciating than going to the stake or the cross, for that were but "a golden step to glory." And I was brought by a process of most intense suffering to experience this death of self, so that I could say, with Paul, "I am crucified with Christ, nevertheless I live; yet not I, but Christ liveth in me." And I knew that my "life was hid with Christ in God."

The language of that sweet hymn commencing,

"Jesus, I my cross have taken,
All to leave, and follow thee,"

was the perfect language of my heart, especially the following lines:

"Go, then, earthly fame and treasure;
Come, disaster, scorn, and pain;
In thy service, pain is pleasure—
With thy favor, loss is gain."

I counted "all things but loss for the excellency of the knowledge of Christ Jesus my Lord." I was satisfied — oh, so abundantly satisfied — with him as my portion.

I was very desirous to win souls to Christ, and constantly live by faith. In endeavoring to accomplish the former, I procured tracts, and went through the tenement-houses where I thought the Saviour was needed. And here I found that "the offence of the cross had not ceased;" but still I labored on, and God blessed my poor efforts.

In reference to the latter—living by faith—the enemy, not a few times, endeavored to wrest my shield from me; and I think the greatest conflicts I ever endured was at such times. He would suggest to me that I was throwing my life away, and sometimes he even dared to tell me that the promises of God were not true. I have sometimes walked for days by naked faith, and without any sensible, joyous emotion, simply using the language: "I WILL believe; I DO believe. It is all true. Heaven and earth shall pass away, but the words of Jesus shall never fail; and those who lose their lives for Christ's sake shall find them again."

I thus learned that the "trial of my faith was more precious than gold;" for, emerging from this state, I invariably was brought out into a large place, and the glory, the ineffable glory, I saw in reserve for those who vanquish the powers of darkness with a "martyr's faith," was beyond all my previous conceptions. Oh, it is true that we should "count it all joy when we fall into divers temptations," and esteem the "trial of our faith more precious than gold;" for "many shall be purified, made white, and" then "tried."

In the enjoyment of this experience I was "kept in perfect peace," for my "mind was stayed on God." I engaged in many labors, not because I thought I could do so much good, but as a faint expression of my love to Jesus.

A long time before this, all fear of death had been taken from me; for I read, "Perfect love casteth out fear." But I must confess that, for some time after I was converted, I had fears which I could not always repress. I suffered much in a thunder-storm, and, before my conversion, would grow sick at the appearance of a coming storm. But from this I was perfectly saved; indeed, I was fully and constantly saved from all fear and anxiety and sin.

When I spoke of this wonderful salvation to others, I found that many did not understand it, who professed to be Christians. I remember once meeting a Christian lady on my tract district, to whom I related my then present experience. I told her that I was "careful for nothing;" that I "prayed without ceasing, rejoiced evermore, and in everything gave thanks;" that I was saved from all my natural tendencies to sin; that I loved God above my chief joy, and had constant fellowship with the Father and the Son and the Holy Spirit; that I knew that the blood of the "Lamb slain from the foundation of the world" had been applied to my sin-stained heart, and had been efficacious in cleansing me, so that I could say I had a clean heart, and that I knew a right spirit, even the blessed Holy Spirit, dwelt within me.

She said, with surprise: "You have received the blessing of sanctification. Oh, how I wish I might enjoy the same!" She was at once brought under conviction for this blessing, and gladly attended the meetings, that she might be taught the perfect way—the "king's highway of holiness."

But this case was an exception. I soon learned that there was much opposition to this glorious doctrine, which to me was so clearly revealed in God's Word.

I have been surprised that professed Christians could endeavor to satisfy themselves without holiness, living quite regardless of the command, "Be ye holy, for I am holy." "Cleanse yourselves from all filthiness of the flesh and spirit, perfecting holiness in the fear of the Lord." I have met many such, in a kind of half-saved state—if such a thing can be—professing a desire to go to heaven, and yet having such an aversion to the doctrine of holiness; hoping one day to see the face of the Lord, and yet opposing the most glorious attribute of his character.

I sought holiness, not because I expected to be rewarded for it, or in order to be happy, but because I regarded the command to be holy as imperative as the command to repent; and I consider salvation inseparably connected with the doctrine of sanctification. It has been my aim to be such a Christian as the Bible demands and as primitive days witnessed. I cannot see any other type of Christianity worthy the name; and I rejoice that there are some who are seeking to lead God's people to this standard.

EXPERIENCE OF REV. A. P. GRAVES,

THE EVANGELIST.

EARLY in life I was the subject of religious impressions. A Christian parentage blessed me, and pious friends sought to instil divine truth into my heart. From my earliest remembrance, family prayer had a most potent influence upon my mind. The effect of those early influences is deep and salutary still. The death of my father, when I was but nine years of age, placed me in a family of strangers, where, for several years, my advantages for religious training were limited.

At times my mind was exercised about my accountability to God, and my need of salvation through the blood of Christ. At length, my soul was deeply wrought upon by the preaching of a Methodist minister of the Wesleyan connection.

I professed conversion and united with the class, and was baptized in the form of that church. For a few months I maintained a nominal profession of religion with a degree of satisfaction, yet was conscious of a leanness. The heart was not tender; it had not been quickened into new life. About five months from my public confession of Christ, I was seized with the deepest convictions of guilt in my soul. I felt that I was lost. I read the Bible, and prayed; but all to no purpose. The wrath of God was abiding upon me; I was under condemnation. My profession had been an empty show; I was self-deceived.

God, in infinite mercy, now showed me my state of heart in sin and guilt. It was Sunday, a beautiful day of sunshine, but all was dark to me. I felt that I was undone; but I said once more: "I will go to Jesus; it is my only hope—

> 'I can but perish if I go;
> I am resolved to try.'"

I again fell prostrate at the feet of Jesus, and out of the bitter depths of my heart cried:

> "Here, Lord, I give myself away;
> 'Tis all that I can do."

And just then Jesus accepted the offering, and spoke peace to my soul. The unspeakable joy I experienced no tongue can tell. I endeavored to tell to the church, to my friends, and the world, what a Saviour I had found. The change I could not mistake. It was the pardoning love of Jesus in the soul; and although my pathway has been varied and crooked from that time until now, I have never, to the present moment, been left to doubt my conversion. In a few months, by yielding to temptation, in an unguarded moment, I fell into a difficulty with one of the brethren of the church, which grieved the Spirit.

My heart became sad, I fainted, and wandered from Christ. I began to live prayerlessly, and to neglect religious meetings. Now began a most wretched experience, which continued nearly three years. I plunged into various schemes of wickedness, chose bad associates for my companions, and often fell into habits of profanity, intemperance, and Sabbath-breaking. But while I inclined to give up Christ, he would not give me up. Frequently did I feel that I was wounding Christ in the house of his friends, and that I was " beaten with many stripes."

At length, I was glad to return to my Father's house. The journey was indeed dark and tedious. Oh, the bitterness, the wrestling, and the agony of my soul in coming back to God! But, blessed be his name, he met me in the way, and threw his arms around my neck and kissed me. And now for more than fifteen years I have taken great delight in the service of Jesus; but not until recently have I believed there were such high attainments by faith and love as are proffered to every Christian who will, by simple "trust" in Jesus, receive the "sealing of the Spirit."

I said I had taken great delight in the service of Christ. Soon after I was reclaimed from my backslidings, I was led by the word of God to see that it was my duty to unite with the Baptist Church, at which time I felt that I was called of God to preach the gospel; and such was my burning love for Jesus, and anxiety for the souls for whom he died, that I cheerfully said, "I will go." I entered a course of study preparatory to the work. Soon my soul seemed to be impressed with the idea that the inclination of the students was to give too much attention to the "letter," and too little attention to the "spirit;" that too little care was taken to have every literary attainment consecrated and sanctified to the great life-work of winning sinners to Christ. I resolved that, whatever acquisition in knowledge I made, all should be laid upon the altar. This blessed resolution and sweet experience I was enabled to carry out as long as I remained in study, and I have felt most deeply its influence upon my ministry.

God has been pleased to crown my labors with constant showers of blessings. But how unworthy I have felt! and, most of all, a deep impression that I had not that confidence in God which it was my privilege to enjoy and my duty to exercise.

In the spring of 1865, after having enjoyed a spiritual refreshing in revivals through the winter, I was impressed, as never before, that there was something in Christ for me which I had never received, and that he was proffering to me the blessing. This conviction was attended with deep searchings of heart; and the more I examined my heart, the more I saw its vileness. My soul was panting for the fulness of Christ's love.

The words of Jesus: "Come unto me, all ye that labor, and are heavy laden, and I will give you rest," came fresh to my mind. "Well," said I, "he spoke them for the sinner, and I have been giving them to the sinner these dozen years; they are not for me." But a voice continually whispered: "They are for *you*." These feelings of desire and trial to do something to satisfy my thirsting soul continued for months. At length, the words above referred to pressed my heart so much, that I began to make a personal application of them. I said: "What is this idea of *rest* as presented by Jesus?" It was thus illustrated to me: Suppose I, wearied from toil, return home and say to my friends: "I am very weary and will retire to rest." I professedly take my bed for this purpose, but spend the night agitated in feeling, with disquiet and tossings. Now, can I rise in the morning, and say I have had *rest?* So it seemed in my soul I had professed to be a Christian, and no doubt had possessed a *good hope*, which has been as an anchor to my soul for many years, but had not *rest*.

Like Martha, I was cumbered about much serving. The waves were rippled; I did not rest by simple trust in Jesus.

I felt deeply conscious that greater heights in spiritual things were attainable; but to reach them was my difficulty. It seemed I would give all the world did I possess it, or do anything if I could but enjoy the fulness of that peace that passeth all understanding.

I tried again and again, with heart, lips, and pen, to consecrate my all to Jesus and his service; and for months my daily cry was: "Oh, for a subdued heart!" But, with all my doing, something would frequently whisper:

> "Cast your deadly doing down—
> Down at Jesus' feet;
> Stand in him, in him alone,
> All glorious and complete."

The labor of my hands at this time greatly increased. Inquiring sinners and rejoicing converts multiplied daily. Never did my ministry seem more responsible or important, and never did I feel so unfit to perform it. I dare not tell any one the state of my own heart. But oh, what trials, as I felt, myself, the sad want of faith that weighed down my soul! When I directed sinners to believe in Christ, some still voice within would say: "Why don't you *believe* yourself?" Again and again I tried to "cast my deadly doing down." I wrote out a full consecration of my all to Jesus, and in solemn prayer signed it upon my knees.

I tried over and over again to examine my heart as with a "lighted candle," but all to no purpose; and I daily found that I was "trying many things of many physicians," and was nothing better, but rather grew worse.

"Oh!" said I, "is it so hard for a Christian to

let go and simply trust Jesus?" After spending several months in deep searchings of heart, a friend put the little tract *The Living Christ* into my hand. The reading of each line awakened increased interest in the matter of believing, trusting. The way appeared plain; but to do the thing was a seeming impossibility. "Oh, for a subdued heart!" was the constant language of my soul. Daily I felt that I could not go and preach to my dear people again; that it was almost wicked to stand up as a public teacher with such a hard, unbroken state of heart.

I determined to appoint a day of fasting and prayer, hoping that by this means I might obtain liberty to my captive soul. I did appoint it; but, thank God, when the time arrived I was compelled to turn it into a day of thanksgiving.

Before my soul deeply panted for the "baptism of the Spirit," I had heard through kind friends of the meeting at Dr. Palmer's, and was invited to attend. I concluded to do so before the appointed day for fasting arrived. I went. The experiences related somewhat illustrated my case. I felt interested, and measured every word. I stated my exercises of mind to the meeting, and was told to try and "trust in Jesus." I said: "I have been trying a long time to believe; but the thing is *to do it.*" Again I fell upon my knees, and endeavored to give up all and "trust," but to no purpose. Still my heart was hard and unrelenting; and again I cried: "Oh, for sweet rest in Jesus!" I felt so unworthy and so rebellious, that I was tempted to conclude that I should never enjoy this blessed experience. But a voice sweetly whispered: "Jesus has promised you the blessing; trust him, accept it."

Wearied, anxious, and still unbelieving, I returned home. While on the way, something seemed to say to me in a most signal tone: "Cast thy burden on the Lord." This precious passage never appeared so to me before. It came as the healing balm. I quickly said: "I will. Lord, if it be selfishness, unholy ambition, worldly pride, the will of man, anything, everything, whatever may hinder my simple 'trust in Jesus,' I surrender all to thee." Still the passage was like a "bright light" before me; and I felt a consciousness that I had cast all at Jesus' feet, and that in his own way and time he would emancipate my burdened soul. I retired to rest, leaving all to him. At an unusually early hour I awoke. The room was silent and dark; but in an instant the darkness passed away, and a bright light filled the room. The light of life seemed to be all around me, and Jesus appeared, not altogether in the form of a person, but as filling the immensity with his presence. I never had such a view of Christ, or experienced such feelings, before. All the hardness of my heart was broken up instantly, and my soul launched out into Christ like launching a boat upon the bosom of a smooth lake. Just now that blessed Scripture: "Bring ye all the tithes into the storehouse, that there may be meat in my house, and prove me now herewith, saith the Lord of hosts, if I will not open you the windows of heaven, and pour out a blessing, that there shall not be room enough to receive it," appeared to me in all its fulness. I said: "I cannot surely contain this." Oh, how my soul was filled with the fulness of Christ's love! The tears freely flowed, and my pillow was wet as with the dew of the morning. Christ was "all in all." "I was filled with the Spirit," and I felt that, after travelling a long and tedious journey over pathless wastes and through burning sands, I had now arrived at the golden gates of the city; yea, had entered and now dwelt in the bright mansions of love. All was peace.

I arose, and made a record of gratitude to God

for his infinite and unspeakable blessing. Immediately I found everything changed concerning my faith in Christ, and my relations to him as a full and complete Saviour.

Never did he appear so much the unchangeable One—"the same yesterday, to-day, and forever." "His yoke became easy, and his burden light;" and, on reflection, I could hardly believe that I had lived and toiled so long without this precious blessing of "sweet rest in Jesus."

I have been led to believe, judging somewhat from appearance, as also from my own experience, that this blessing is the great want of the church *now;* that all alike, ministers and laymen, imperatively need the baptism of the Spirit, and power from on high, that they may convincingly and with conquering power witness for Jesus.

> "Ye need no learning of the schools
> To prove your faith divine."

Witnessing from the heart is the *world's great need.* Let Christians everywhere consecrate themselves to the great work of bringing out the experience and power, and pointing to the ultimate end of the "inner life of Christ in the soul," and the whole aspect of evangelizing the world will change.

EXPERIENCE OF MRS. J. H.

IT was in the early part of June, 1861, that I was led by the Holy Spirit to give my heart to God, and become a follower of the Lord Jesus Christ. From my earliest childhood I had been surrounded by Christian influences, but being naturally of a gay and lively disposition, passionately fond of worldly amusements, I broke away from all Christian and home influence, in order to gratify my natural tastes, and, until I was twenty years of age, was one of Satan's most devoted followers.

My dear mother's prayers followed me, however, during all this time, for ever and anon I would hear the voice of the gentle Spirit urging me to give my heart to God. I would answer: "Yes, but not now — not now; at some future time, when I get older, and have become satiated with the pleasures of the world." Ah, how unsatisfying they were, even then. How often, when whirling in the giddy dance, memories of my childhood's home and of my mother's grief—did she know how I was engaged—would sadden my heart, and in a moment destroy all my anticipated pleasure! In the midst of scenes of earthly enjoyment my soul was ever yearning after purer and more lasting joys, and as year after year rolled on I became more and more dissatisfied with the transient pleasures of the world, but knew not how to better my condition. I used to think: "Oh, how I wish I was a true Christian;" but always felt deeply sensible of my own inability to become one.

Dark days came, however—oh, such days, and weeks, and months, and even years, of sadness and gloom; every cup of earthly happiness was embittered, and I was utterly wretched. I knew not what to do, nor where to look for help. I had grieved away the Holy Spirit time and again; I had poured contempt upon God's love, and would not have him to reign over me; and now, when dark days had come and all earthly sources of joy had failed, he had forsaken me. For two long years I sought the Saviour sorrowing. My sins, oh, how they haunted me day and night! I hardly dared close my eyes in sleep, for fear I should wake in hell. My friends wondered at the change in my appearance, but attributed it to physical debility. They recommended a physician. I took his prescriptions, but they did me no good; none but the great Physician of sin-sick souls could cure my malady; and he did—blessed, ever blessed be his name.

I cannot tell when I first exercised faith in Christ. I remember one Sabbath afternoon taking my Testament, and as I read page after page of the sacred word, oh, what sweetness there seemed in it, what food for my hungry soul! What a different book it was! I wondered it had never seemed so interesting before. I felt like a person who had suddenly found some great treasure, and I thought I should never grow weary of reading. How I longed to tell some one what I had found; but I did not, and for two or three weeks I kept my new-found joy locked up in my own breast, until, one Saturday evening, I was invited to attend the young ladies' prayer-meeting connected with the church of which I am now a member.

At the close of the meeting, the pastor asked me if I was a professor of religion. I replied, "No." He then asked me if I had ever met with a change of heart. I immediately replied: "I believe I have during the past few weeks." And oh! I shall never forget what a flood of light and joy rushed into my soul and through my whole being as I thus gave expression to my faith in Christ. From that night I had no doubt as to the genuineness of my conversion. The Spirit himself bore witness with my spirit, that I was born of God; and shortly after I related my experience and united with the church of my choice, not without meeting with opposition, however, from those whom I loved very dearly, on account of my particular views in regard to baptism. But God gave me grace to walk in the path of duty, with his word alone for my guide, and the language of my heart constantly was: "You may have the world, only give me Jesus." On the third Sunday in July, 1861, I was buried with Christ in baptism, and raised to walk in a new life indeed; a life of peace and joy, such as the world cannot give nor take away. Oh! how I exult in the thought, that we can be placed in no position in life where we may not rejoice in the Lord.

About two months after my conversion, my thoughts were very specially directed to the subject of sanctification, by attending a grove meeting held purposely for the benefit of those who were seeking that experience. I did not go as a seeker of sanctification particularly; but, when the invitation was given for those who desired an experience of that kind to manifest it by rising, I at once arose. I knew there could be no blessing in the Christian life above my aspirations. I always used to think, when an unconverted sinner, "If ever I become a Christian I will be a whole-hearted one." I did not stop to consider whether I was worthy of enjoying the experience of sanctification. I only knew that the word of God demanded, in view of the sufferings and death of Christ on the cross for me, that I should present my body a living sacrifice, holy and acceptable unto God, which was but my reasonable service; and while I thus met his requirements, Christ was made unto me wisdom, righteousness, sanctification, and redemption. I at once made an entire consecration of myself to God then and there; and without any effort on my part, just simply believed that Jesus was all to me that he had promised to be.

I did not have an opportunity of bearing my testimony that day, but a few days afterward I did, in a meeting in the city; and oh, how God blessed me! My soul was filled with joy unutterable in thus honoring Christ by simply believing the truth of his word. From that time I breathed as it were the very atmosphere of heaven.

> "Jesus, all the day long,
> Was my joy and my song."

Trials the most bitter and severe had no power to destroy my happiness. My mind was constantly stayed on God, and he kept me in perfect peace according to his promise; and if ever I have lived devoid of that peace during the intervening time, it has been on account of my lack of faith in Jesus. He is unchangeable, the same yesterday, to-day, and forever. Blessed, ever blessed be the name of Jesus, it is my privilege to abide in him as the branch abideth in the vine, and constantly to bring forth fruit to the honor and glory of his name, who hath called me from darkness into his marvellous light, and from the bondage of sin into the glorious liberty of the children of God.

EXPERIENCE OF JOHN Q. ADAMS,

PASTOR IN NEW YORK CITY.

MY first impressions on the subject of religion must have been received at a very early age, as I can remember scarcely anything anterior to them. When I was six years of age I was deeply impressed with a sense of my sins in the sight of God, and my unfitness for death, by an address made to a Sunday-school where I occasionally attended—as the Presbyterian church, of which my widowed mother was a member, and where I usually went to Sunday-school, was at considerable distance from our residence. I was frequently very much troubled, and, at times, deeply affected in reading the Holy Scriptures, especially the story of the cross. This would often melt me to tears. When I was about ten years of age, I was led, one Saturday morning, in school, under a deeper sense of my guilt than I had ever felt before, to utter the prayer of the publican: "God be merciful to me, a sinner." I felt that God heard and answered my petition. Peace and joy such as I had never known before filled my soul. But I had no one to guide and teach me. I was but a child, and quite small for my age; and there was much skepticism in the church I attended about the conversion of children. I took great delight in the means of grace, and especially the prayer meetings, which I regularly attended. My peace and joy wore away, and I did not think this was conversion until years afterward, when God taught me more fully by his word and Spirit.

When I was about closing my twelfth year I left my native city, Philadelphia, and came to reside in New York, among strangers. I was almost without restraint, except that which my Heavenly Father imposed by his special providence and grace. I was scrupulously moral, but in a legal spirit, and therefore always more or less under condemnation. When about sixteen I learned to dance, and then the ball-room and the theatre were frequent places of resort, until, at length, I secured an engagement to perform with a celebrated pantomime company, in one of the fashionable gardens in New York city. During all this time, however, God kept me from the vices so almost universally prevalent among this class. From intemperance, gambling, and licentiousness, I was almost miraculously preserved. I still attended church regularly on the Lord's day, and flattered myself that I was as good as the majority of professed Christians—many of whom I used to see at the garden through the week, and at the church on Sunday.

When I was nearly twenty years of age I began to think very seriously of devoting myself to the service of God; it seemed to me very reasonable and proper that I should do so. Circumstances led me to attend the ministrations of Rev. George Benedict, pastor of the Norfolk Street Baptist church, and I began to read the Bible. I soon found that "I must be born again." The holiness of God, the justice and extent of the law, my own unworthiness and helplessness and ruin were now set before me in such a way that I began to despair of salvation. I read of Christ, and thought of Christ as a Saviour. "But surely," I thought, "he cannot, he will not save a wretch so vile as I am." I had no kind friend to whom I could go and tell my troubles.

At length, I got a friend to make an appointment for me with Pastor Benedict. The conversation was much blest to my soul. I saw that the Holy Spirit was showing me my own guilt and depravity that I might be compelled to abandon my self-righteousness, and trust only in Jesus for justification before God. I left my pastor and went to my room, and there cast myself unreservedly upon the mercy of God in Christ, and received the witness of the Spirit that my sins were all forgiven, and that I was adopted into the family of God. Oh, the joy that filled my soul! I was in an ecstasy of delight. I could only say, "Praise the Lord!" "Oh, *my* Father!"—repeating these words, while my whole frame quivered with the sweet rapture that thrilled my soul. I soon after made a public profession of religion, by baptism, and united with the Norfolk Street Baptist church.

When about twenty-one years of age I yielded to convictions which had long been pressing upon me, and began a course of preparation for the gospel ministry, in Madison University. The loss of what little I had saved soon made it necessary for me to return to New York, and I entered a classical school there. I was now nearly twenty-two years old. My experience, hitherto, had been of that vacillating character so generally prevalent among Christians; but, about this time, I was sweetly led by the Holy Spirit to rely on Jesus every moment. He was an ever-present reality to me; my constant companion, in every place and at every moment. He saved me—fully saved me. I had no one to teach me that it was my privilege to continue in this blessed experience by the exercise of simple faith in Jesus; but supposed, from what I heard of the experience of others, and from the preaching to which I listened, that I was enjoying a special season of mercy which I must not expect to continue. This sweet state I enjoyed for about two months, as nearly as I now can remember; exactly how I lost it I cannot tell; but I know that I again began to experience doubts and fears, and to be overcome by temptation, and mourn the absence of my Saviour, and have an experience like the rest of my brethren in these respects. But I could not now be satisfied with this. I felt a conviction that there must be something better for the Christian.

Very powerful temptations were now assailing me, and I heard a great deal of self-examination, and of being faithful, and of watching and praying, but very little about believing. I used to pray a great deal, and watch, and make vows, and struggle against my inbred corruptions and outward temptations; but, oh! how often, almost constantly, I was living under bondage to sin. I found my own strength to be perfect weakness. I went on sinning and repenting, "resolving and re-resolving," and yet with the gloomy prospect of "dying the same." During all this time, however, I cherished a lively faith in Christ as my justification before God, and constantly repaired to the throne of grace, and rested on the prevalence of his intercession as my Advocate with the Father. But, oh! how I looked, and sometimes longed for death, to set me free from my sins And yet, the thought would often press itself upon my attention: "Will death make you holy? Death will not affect the soul. It will, indeed, remove you from the temptations from without which assail you here; but how can it remove your inbred sin?" And then, in my struggles, I would sometimes be reminded of some of the precious promises of God's Word, and it seemed that there must be deliverance and rest and triumph in this life. I read (1 Cor. 10 : 13), "There hath no temptation taken you but such as is common to man; but God is faithful, who will not suffer you to be tempted above that ye are able; but will, with the temptation, also make a way to escape, that ye may be able to bear it." Also (Phil. 4 : 13), "I can do all things through Christ who strengtheneth me;" which was the first text I ever preached from. I also read (Eph. 3 : 20), that God was "able to do exceeding abundantly above all we ask or think," and (John 14 : 13, 14) "Whatsoever ye ask in my (Christ's) name, that will I do, that the Father may be glorified in the Son. If ye shall ask anything in my name, I will do it." From the day on which I experienced pardon, I had been led to pray that I might be "holy, humble, and useful;" and when, overcome by temptation, I fell into sin, oh! how earnest were my prayers to be kept from again falling. I could "ask" to be saved from sin—I could "think" of being a holy, humble servant of Christ, in a sense beyond that which I then experienced; and the Word told me that God was able to do "exceeding abundantly above" that, and that Christ *would* do for me whatsoever I asked in his name.

Here, then, was God's own declaration that he was able and willing to do all I needed to have done. Let it be borne in mind that, during all these exercises, my experience of justification was clear, and though, at times, the adversary would suggest to me that I was not converted, and that I would be cast off and left to perish, I always met him with the reply: "I trust in Christ to save me (when I come to die, was the idea of being saved then), and I will not doubt his ability or willingness to do it, though I am the chief of sinners." It was not salvation from the wrath of God I longed for, but salvation from sin. Not from its guilt, but from its pollution; not from its punishment, but from its dominion and power. And yet I was in bondage.

This experience continued until the year 1856. Meanwhile I had entered the ministry. My labors were multiplied. I determined to do all that it was possible to do in the service of Christ, and shrank not from any burden; and, though illy qualified to preach (speaking after the manner of men), yet I was always ready to "stand up for Jesus;" but often with great nervousness and doubt and fear. I was "in labors more abundant." If salvation from sin had been by working, I certainly think I should have obtained it.

On the first of January, 1856, I assumed the

pastoral charge of the North Baptist church, New York city. A young member of the church, whom I baptized on the first Sunday of that year, one day came to me with a glowing description of a meeting which he had been providentially led to attend. From what he said of it, I told him that I guessed he had been to a Methodist perfection meeting. He assured me that he heard nothing but Jesus exalted, and the brethren and sisters confessing that they were only sinners saved by grace. I at length determined that I would go and see for myself what kind of a meeting it was. I went more from curiosity than anything else. I expected to detect a great deal of arrogance and self-exaltation in the remarks of the speakers. On entering the room— it was the front parlor in a private residence—I was very solemnly impressed. However it may sound to others, it seemed to me that the very atmosphere in that room was different from any I had ever breathed. Over the mantelpiece this motto was suspended in a plain, gilt frame: "Holiness unto the Lord." I was filled with awe, and at once silently breathed an earnest prayer that God would bless the meeting to me and to all.

Before the opening services were concluded, all

my curiosity was gone. I was there as a learner. I found a good Baptist brother there with whom I was acquainted, and who was acquainted with most of those present. The company numbered about twenty. As one after another rose to speak, my friend whispered to me: "That's a Presbyterian; that's a Congregationalist; that's a Methodist; that's an Episcopalian; that's a Quaker; that's a Baptist." I was surprised and delighted. Here were persons connected with six or seven of the different denominations, all speaking one language, and all bound together in the most fervent Christian love. Christ, a full and complete Saviour, a present Saviour from all sin, was the theme. Here was the experience for which I had longed. I was irresistibly carried back to the time when I enjoyed this blessing, but did not know it by the name of "sanctification," or indeed by any name. But the reality of it I could not doubt. I arose and told of my former experience, and of my present struggles. I attended this meeting only about four times, with intervals between my visits to it, and then circumstances transpired which prevented my further attendance upon it, or at least I thought so. I was led, however, to see that the way to retain the experience which I once possessed, was to live by the moment—or, in other words, to look every moment to Christ. This was of great service to me. I was led also to make a very full consecration of myself and all I had to the service of God, as follows:

My Heavenly Father: Recognizing the reasonableness of thy commands, and the benevolence of thy designs in making provision so abundant for the holiness of thy people, and earnestly desiring the entire sanctification of all my powers to thy service and glory, humbly relying on the merits of thy dear Son, my blessed Saviour, for acceptance in this act, I do now solemnly and for ever consecrate to thee all that I am and all that I have.

I give to thee, to be made holy to thyself, my frail, weak body, with all its members and all their capacities.

I consecrate to thee my soul, with all its faculties—my affections, understanding, judgment, will, conscience, memory—my ability to think, speak, and act as a rational creature.

I devote my spirit, with all its perceptions.

I consecrate body, soul, and spirit, O Lord, to thee.

I lay upon thine altar all my attainments and all my possessions.

Whatever thou hast made me steward of, I consecrate to thee; praying that thou wilt sanctify me wholly, and give me grace ever hereafter to live for thy glory alone, and that, for Christ's sake, thou will accept me. Amen.
New York, July 30, 1856.

I lived in this consecrated state about two years, during which time I was abundant in pastoral labors, and the blessing of the Lord in an unusual degree rested upon the church. Still I was not delivered from the power and dominion of sin. I sought grace to perform my part of the covenant, but did not believe that God performed *his* part. I gave all to God to be sanctified to his service; but I failed to believe that for Christ's sake he did so sanctify all to himself. I was therefore at times still overcome by sin—though in the main satisfied with the blessings which God was conferring upon me, and with what I considered my own progress. I was settling down into the conclusion that sanctification was not a distinct work or experience in the soul.

But how strangely God works! In the summer of 1858 I was attacked with dysentery, and did not know but that I was about to be called home. I thought it would be a pleasant thing to fall asleep in Jesus, if my work was done. But it pleased my heavenly Father to restore me to health again. And now comes a period of my history which I would fain blot out. Instead of devoting myself renewedly to God and presenting my prolonged life as a sacrifice upon God's altar, I became neglectful of my spiritual interests, yielded to temptation, and fell into sin. During this time, I did not dare to read my act of consecration, but whenever I found it among my papers, I would hastily put it aside or cover it up.

This state of things lasted about five months, during which time the work of grace in the church began to decline; awakenings were less frequent; young converts became worldly, and no power attended the word. This alarmed me. I felt that I was the cause of it all. My sin of backsliding appeared most aggravated, and bitterly before God did I repent. He graciously heard my cries, and gave me pardon. Again his blessing rested upon my labors; and thus I entered the year 1859.

But I was not now satisfied with my experience. I felt that I needed not only pardon, but cleansing; not only justification, but sanctification. I now had such views of my natural depravity as

I never had before; I saw myself such a sinner that I loathed and abhorred myself. But I did not now look for death to set me free. Nay, I could not desire death, as I had done, while in this state. I began to look to Jesus, not to death, as my entire and complete sanctification, as my full Saviour from sin. But, oh! what struggles now ensued! I was endeavoring to overcome sin, to sanctify myself, before I came to Jesus.

I began now to preach a higher Christian experience. My preaching of Christian morality had always been up to the New Testament standard, so that many thought me unnecessarily strict in my views on this point; but I now saw that the failure on my own part to exemplify that standard, and my failure to lead my people to live up to it, was owing to the want of a corresponding experience in my own heart, and, consequently, the lack of clear teaching of such an experience to them.

As the result of this preaching, a young lady, a member of the church, became convicted of her need of a better experience, and came to tell the exercises of her soul to me, and ask for direction. I could not direct her. She was as far advanced as I was. We were both under conviction. Her visit made a deep impression upon my mind.

Here was I, a pastor, unable to lead one of my own flock forward in the divine life. I began to feel more and more deeply my need—my nothingness. Language cannot describe the emotions of my soul. Oh, how ignorant I felt myself; how empty—how vile and worthless. I thought that my sinfulness kept me from receiving strength and full salvation. I began to agonize in prayer, spending hours together upon my knees. I fasted and prayed and wept; but oh, how strange, I did not *believe*—I could not.

During this time the Lord was again blessing my labors in the conversion of souls. Anxious inquirers frequently came to see me. In conversing with them I used to urge them to *believe* in Jesus. I used to say, after hearing their confessions of sin and helplessness: "Well, you see that you are lost, and you cannot save yourself, and you know that none but Jesus can save you; now why do you not believe his word? Cast yourself upon him and believe." And it would seem as though the Holy Spirit would echo back to my soul: "And why do not *you* believe? you know you are vile and helpless, and Jesus only can cleanse and sanctify you: why do you not cast yourself on him and believe?" I could only breathe out the prayer, "Lord, help us to believe." On the fourth day of March, 1859, I appended the following to the act of consecration above quoted :

"Having carefully read the above, I do again renew this consecration, in the presence of the Great Searcher of hearts."

Following this, there were deep searchings of the heart. It seemed to me that everything I held dear was separately presented to me, and the question propounded: "Can you part with this for Jesus?"

Then would come the suggestion: "If you *do* give these things to the Lord, he will take them from you, in order to test the sincerity of the consecration." In this way, my wife, my only child, my property, the church of which I was pastor, my reputation as a preacher, a Christian and a man, my influence, my official station as a minister, and everything to which the heart naturally clings, were presented to me with the question: "Can you part with this for Jesus? Are you willing that God should take this from you, if it is for his glory?" God, by the power of his Spirit, whose help I sought, enabled me to say, "Yea, Lord, strip me of all, if thou wilt but cleanse me from sin and use me only for thy glory." And there, in my study, I passed through the mental struggle of a separation from all that I once called mine—now no longer mine, but God's—laid upon the altar, a whole burnt offering to the Lord. I now knew what it was to be "crucified unto the world," "crucified with Christ." I felt now that my consecration was no sham—it was a reality; and I praised God that he had enabled me thus to give him his own. But, oh! how insignificant, how worthless my offering appeared. There was nothing in it meritorious; I was but an unprofitable servant. Yet I hoped for acceptance through Jesus Christ.

But could I *believe* that so unworthy an offering was accepted? Not yet. About this time I began again to attend the meetings for the promotion of holiness; and I here learned that after all was given *to* Christ, it was the privilege of faith to have all *in* Christ; but yet I dared not believe. I was also looking for some *sensible* evidence that my sacrifice was accepted. I expected an *emotional* experience like that which thrilled my soul, and body too, when I received Christ as my justification. And so, when I was praying and *trying* to believe, the adversary was constantly directing my attention to myself, and asking, " Do you *feel* different?" Thus I was kept for some weeks in bondage to unbelief.

On the morning of March 22, while spending several hours on my knees, the following promises were presented in succession at intervals to my mind:—"Ask and ye shall receive; seek and ye shall find; knock and it shall be opened unto you." "All things whatsoever ye shall ask in prayer believing, ye shall receive." "What things soever ye desire when ye pray, believe that ye receive them, and ye shall have them." "There standeth one among you who baptizeth with the Holy Spirit." "Bind the sacrifice with cords, even to the horns of the altar." "Him who is able to do exceeding abundantly above all that we can ask or think"—in connection with, "All things whatsoever ye shall ask in prayer believing, ye shall receive." These promises came into my mind at intervals during two or three hours of earnest prayer. But I arose from my knees, still in unbelief, and consequently unblest.

Two days after (the 24th), as I was about to retire, I looked up to God, and asked him to direct me to a portion of his word which would enlighten me. I opened the Bible to this text: "Abraham *believed* God" (there seemed to be a peculiar emphasis on the word "believed"), "and it was counted to him for righteousness." I then began to trust, without any feeling or emotion. I resigned myself to sleep and awoke the next morning, wholly trusting in the Lord.

It was on that day, the 25th of March, that I cast myself wholly upon Jesus as my sanctification, and realized by faith that his blood cleansed me from all sin. I was in prayer in my study. The text of the preceding evening, "Abraham believed God," etc., came powerfully into my mind.

I seemed to be led thus: "I have given all to God for the express purpose that all may be sanctified to himself; I have given myself to him that I may be cleansed from all sin. I will ask and believe." I felt that the power to believe was given me by the Holy Spirit. I no longer looked to myself—to my emotions, or feelings, but to the promise—and I *dared* to say, "I believe that the blood of Jesus Christ *does now* cleanse *me* from *all* sin." All within was calm as a summer's eve. No ecstasy or rapture *disturbed* the deep peace which filled my soul, as I experienced the consciousness that it was even so.

That day was a day of *peace*, such as I had never

enjoyed before. Oh, it seemed so easy to trust all in the hands of Jesus. I was nothing—Jesus was all, and I was content that it should be so. But, oh what a Saviour I felt Jesus to be now. Through him I was more than a conqueror. Sin had no dominion over me. I had no anxiety, no fear; Jesus fully saved me, and saved me fully each moment. I entered into rest—the rest of faith; and soon my soul was filled to overflowing with the love of Christ, and praise filled my heart and burst forth from my lips.

More than ten years have now rolled away, and oh, what a history they have! I have realized more of the goodness of God, and the power of Jesus to save during that time, than during all my previous history combined. Trials such as I never before endured have come upon me; tests of faith have been applied by my heavenly Father; but oh, his grace *is* sufficient, and Jesus *has* saved, and *does* save me. And amid the fiercest assaults of the tempter, and the severest trials, I have sung songs of praise to Jesus, and he has put to flight the armies of the aliens, and cheered me with his presence and smile. I give myself to him that he may glorify himself in me, and I just believe that he does it. I simply

"into nothing fall,
That Jesus may be all in all."

"I am crucified with Christ, nevertheless I live: yet not I, but Christ liveth in me; and the life I now live in the flesh I live by the faith of the Son of God, who loved me and gave himself for me." Hallelujah. Amen.

EXPERIENCE OF MRS. A. H.

IN my childhood I was brought up in the school of severely cold religious discipline, and my religious habits were consequently formed under a sense of duty. No religious form that belongs to a well-ordered family was neglected. Regular attendance at church and stated hours for Scripture reading and prayer were scrupulously observed.

Being of an enthusiastic nature, the mellow tones of a grand organ, with the delicious strains of well-trained voices, had equal charms for me on the Sabbath with the lighter music of the opera on week days, and the well-turned periods of a gifted speaker were to me as pleasing as any performance of a less grave character.

According to the custom of the Episcopal church, I was prepared, at the age of fourteen, for the rite of confirmation; and, so far as I knew at that time, I possessed a fair sense of the misery and shame which every child of wrath (according to the teaching of that church) is expected to bear for himself or herself. I felt myself, truly, a miserable sinner, condemned by own conscience and the Word of God, yet hoping for salvation through grace and good works. As it was not deemed essential by my religious instructors, among whom was the curate of the parish, that I should know more than this, I presented myself at the altar. The ceremony was solemn and affected me seriously. I was humbled, and yearned for closer communion with God. But I had to be satisfied with emotional, evanescent piety, springing rather from the effect of the touching scene surrounding me than from any change wrought in my heart.

As I had never been taught that there was sin in attending balls, theaters, or other genteel places of amusement, I never for a moment thought of giving them up, nor, indeed, of making any sacrifice of time or inclination to the service of God. Thus I passed many years—a member of the church and yet a worldling.

At the age of twenty-two I was attacked with a weakness of the optic nerve, which confined me some weeks to a dark room. During this period of imprisonment I realized, for the first time, the difference between an intellectual apprehension of God and a personal, saving faith in Christ. God's Spirit strove with me, and revealed to me the impurity of my heart, and then I saw that it was a fountain of iniquity. I searched my soul, and found it was desperately wicked. The life I had led looked dark and terrible. I bemoaned, with sincere contrition, the sins of my whole life, and began to think seriously of bringing this sinful heart into subjection. I looked upon it as a lifelong work, and almost shrank from such a task as hopeless. I implored divine aid to assist me to clear up the darkness of my way; and oh, if I had known at that time some better teaching than that I had received, how much easier might have been my way! how much self-torture and trembling and anxiety, and how many false steps might I have been spared!

I turned to the Word of God prayerfully, and tremblingly paused over the great work of atonement. How it could affect *me*, so unworthy, seemed a mystery inexplicable. "I will give up the world," I said; "I will subdue self; I will do God's will, and then I will bring my good works as an offering, and God shall bless me." Fully persuaded that God's law must be my rule of life, and that in keeping it I would daily become more like the ideal formed in my own mind of a true Christian, I left that dark room, having had a glimpse of Canaan, without, alas! knowing how to reach it.

With the return of health came carelessness and forgetfulness of my resolutions. I went into the world again, but it could no longer hold me with its fascinations. The frivolity of the thoughtless ceased to attract me, and I turned with earnest desire to find rest in Him who is ready to forgive and plenteous in mercy unto all them that call upon him. I could say:

> "Mercy, good Lord, mercy I seek:
> This is the total sum;
> Mercy through Christ is all my suit,
> Lord, let thy mercy come."

I was convicted of sin, and more than ever cast down; and having no real spiritual adviser, no true Christian friend to lead me, strange as it may seem to the reader, I resolved, in this my hour of anguish, to repeat my vows of confirmation. This resolution was based on the conviction that I was not actuated by proper motives, and had failed to do, in deed and in truth, what I had done only in form.

In the spring of 1859, I became interested in a young girl, who was preparing for confirmation, and, in a very imperfect manner, sought to assist her. While thus engaged, her simple and clear apprehension of the plan of redemption surprised and impressed me. Seriously and prayerfully I repaired to the church where the rite of confirmation was to be administered, not as a candidate, but alone. Apart, and in the lowest depths of humiliation, I cried for mercy, and release from sin. The agony of that hour words cannot tell. It was the agony of a guilty sinner before her judge, pleading for her very life; and, oh! blessed be his name, God, in the fulfilment of his word, graciously heard and answered that prayer. Jesus appeared to me for the first time as *my* Saviour, and these words, "I am the way and the truth and the life," came forcibly to my mind, followed by the blessed text: "The blood of Jesus Christ, his Son, cleanseth from all sin." I then knew that

> "Tears, tho' flowing like a river,
> Never can one sin efface;
> Jesus' tears would not avail thee;
> Blood alone can meet thy case.
> Fly to Jesus,
> Life is found in His embrace."

Yes, I had found refuge in Jesus—in his blood. The scales of unbelief fell from my eyes; my sin-sick soul was washed in the blood of Jesus, and then and there I stood—the confirmation ceremony over—enjoying peace in believing. Time cannot efface the precious remembrance of that moment.

Oh, how changed was everything now. "Old things had passed away, and, behold! all things had become new." How great was my delight in studying—*not reading*—the Word. The agony in the garden, the crucifixion on Calvary, and every event in the Saviour's life seemed to have a new and a deeper significance to me.

Much as I then rejoiced in my new-found experience of a death unto sin and a life unto righteousness, I have learned by a later experience that I was then but a babe in Christ. But I was full of joy; my cup would hold no more. To serve God, to live in his fear and in his love, was my purpose. I had found access to him through Christ, the living way. I had lost all confidence in self—all dependence on works. I yielded myself up to God, and enjoyed a clear evidence of justification by faith in Jesus. Days and weeks of holy joy passed by; and thus, for four years, I walked in the steady light of an unwavering trust.

But, alas! shame and confusion fill me as I recount my sad fall from this life of simple, happy faith in God. And yet at the same time, I call upon my soul to bless and magnify his name for his goodness towards me; for, but for this fall, appalling though it was, and deeply humiliating, my soul would perhaps never have known the great depths of God's love. As the deepest waters roll beside the highest mountains, so often do the richest blessings of God linger behind his darkest frowns. I was tried, deeply tried; and the burden which the Lord laid upon me seemed too hard for me to bear. I rebelled. My lot was too burdensome. A husband with whom I had enjoyed for ten years the highest domestic felicity, suddenly manifested symptoms of an impaired intellect. The shock was so unexpected and overwhelming that for a time I sank under it. "Is God a consuming fire? Is he angry with his people every day?" I inquired. And then, in the language of David, I would exclaim: "Oh, that I had wings like a dove, that I might fly away and be at rest." Oh, for some haven of security against the conflict of sin, the weakness of the flesh, the trials of life, and the frowns of Providence.

For six months I lived estranged from God, and

in violation of my consecration vows, belonging neither to heaven with its rest, nor to earth with its pleasures; a wretched, storm-tossed soul, without a compass or a helm, driven before the waves. At the end of those dark months, I sought the Lord with tears and groans. My soul struggled as it had never done before. I poured out my soul in prayer, and in utter self-abnegation I pleaded the righteousness of Christ. My will was subdued, and I could say:

> "It is the Lord; shall I resist,
> Or contradict his will,
> Who cannot do but what is just,
> And must be righteous still?"

I then inquired of myself: "Why this failure in my Christian course? Why this 'fall from grace'?" I felt there was a want in my soul which had never yet been supplied. I longed to know of some power to *save* me, some power to *keep* me from sin. I prayed fervently, I prayed often, and felt very, very near to God, when suddenly a voice seemed to whisper: "Give thyself and all thou hast to God," and, as if moved by an almighty power, I obeyed. I consecrated myself, my husband, my children, my all. I withheld nothing from my God; and thenceforth I held all as the

Lord's. My duty seemed now more clear, my path more bright. The floodgates of God's love opened upon me. I pause, even now, in solemn awe, as I recall the peace which took possession of my soul. It was more than the joy of salvation; it was a holy calm within, "the peace of God which passeth understanding." It was not, however, until I had surrendered self wholly, and consecrated everything fully, that this rich blessing, this happy experience was mine. The lesson was hard to learn, but, having learned it, it yields rich fruit. "Take my yoke," says our Saviour, "and learn of me, for I am meek and lowly; and ye shall find rest to your souls."

Very soon the grace given was tested. In the providence of God I was called to pass through deep waters of affliction, lasting many months; yet my soul rested firmly on Christ. I knew his strength was imparted to me, enabling me to do and to suffer his good pleasure. Sickness and death of dear loved ones were trying my faith, but it wavered not nor doubted. I could see beloved ones pass into the silence of the grave without a murmur; I could behold my home made desolate by the death of my husband and children, and still sing songs of praise; and, amid the wreck of earthly hopes and ambitions, I could look beyond all to Jesus, and realize his strength to sustain and his presence to cheer me.

Thus far I had no human teaching in reference to the doctrine of sanctification. My attention was first called to it by the preaching of a series of six sermons on that subject by the pastor of a Baptist church in New York City, in March, 1865.

The last sermon, from Job 35 : 3—" What profit shall I have if I be cleansed from my sin?" —interested me deeply, not as presenting anything new in my experience, but in *precisely describing what I had already experienced.* I rejoiced that my own views had been fully expressed by another. Oh, what unspeakable joy filled my soul, as I realized that the Spirit, who had been searching my heart and discovering to me my guilt and vileness, and my need of a perfect Saviour, had also fixed the seal of his approbation upon me by revealing Jesus unto me, not only as my justification, but also as my sanctification. I had therefore learned and proved this doctrine, not by first hearing of it from human lips, and then seeking it, but I had learned it by conflict with nature and its passions, by fighting the powers of darkness, by struggling against sin, and by triumph through faith in Jesus, the mighty Conqueror.

The stream of sanctifying grace having flowed into my soul, to enjoy more of this saving power now became my chief desire. I sought further guidance and light by reading books on that subject, and comparing them with the word of God. I also read the experiences of godly and devoted men and women; and was much helped by attending the Baptist church above referred to, where the doctrine of sanctification was prominently presented. This hungering after righteousness and true holiness could only be satisfied with the enjoyment of Jesus as my all in all; and I was not disappointed in so seeking him. He met me in the way —he extended to me the fulness of his love. He enabled me to trust him fully and enter into sweet and abiding rest.

Hitherto I had been in bondage to the ritualism of the Episcopal church. It was not until I felt the freedom which flows from fully comprehending and appropriating Christ, as my perfect and all-sufficient Saviour, that I saw how these forms had trammelled me. I began to feel that I was hindered by these forms in getting to Jesus; and with the increase of light and liberty came the desire to be freed from these trammels. I was greatly tried at this point. Many objections were presented to discourage and perplex, but faith would have nothing but Jesus; and after deliberation and prayer, encouraged by the example of Rev. Baptist W. Noel, whose experience had been somewhat similar to mine, I resolved to throw off these fetters.

The study of God's word fully convinced me that the immersion of a believer on confession of faith in Jesus was the only Scriptural baptism, and without entering into the discussion of this subject, on which much might be said, I simply state I presented myself as a candidate for membership in a Baptist church in New York, was accepted, and submitted publicly to the command of Jesus. The ordinance was much blessed to me. "In keeping his commands there is great reward"—the reward of an approving conscience; the reward of receiving more light, in proportion as we sink into the will of God.

The possession of this sweet and blessed experience of entire sanctification sheds a holy calm around me at all times. Amid the keenest disappointments, and in the lesser trials of everyday life, a constant peace possesses me, and even when not engaged in active devotions my soul continually enjoys holy communion with God, and thus life, with me, is prayer, and prayer is life. One of the blessed phases of this experience is the power, through grace, to overcome. "I can do all things through Christ, which strengtheneth me." Phil. 4: 13. Entire sanctification elevates the human into a conscious union with the divine. A constant stream of ineffable peace flows into my heart, filling my entire being with sweet delight. Momentary triumphs over self and sin evince the constant presence and power of Jesus. I speak to him as to a familiar friend, and his name is almost constantly breathed in holy joy. I feel a deep interest in the conversion of souls, a longing desire to be more useful in the cause of Christ, and to that end I consecrate my whole being. No terror alarms, no doubts disturb me. Death inspires no fear. If there are new heights to be reached, my soul aspires to them, for, in the language of the Apostle, I can say: "This one thing I do, forgetting those things which are behind, and, reaching forth unto those things which are before, I press toward the mark, for the prize of the high calling of God in Christ Jesus."

EXPERIENCE OF C. W. BROOKS,

PASTOR IN BROOME CO., N. Y.

THE apostle exhorts us to "be ready to give to every one that asketh a reason of the hope that is in us, with meekness and fear." I would therefore confess what God has done for my soul, in leading it from the dark and dreary wilderness of sin into the land that flows with milk and honey. Although I am unable to see anything very peculiar or striking in my experience that has not been realized by a multitude of others, yet, under the blessing of God, it may encourage those who are seeking to know the full and perfect salvation of Christ from all sin.

From my earliest recollection, I was the subject of strong religious impressions, and often inwardly resolved to become a Christian. I often thought that to be a true Christian would be the maximum of all happiness in this life, and, therefore, I desired to experience the power of religion. I do not now remember that any other motive operated upon my mind to induce me to seek the salvation of my soul till I was in my fourteenth year, when it pleased God to show me the exceeding sinfulness of my heart. I was alarmed, and for the first time I began in real earnestness to seek salvation from sin. Before, I only wished to escape hell; now, I wanted to get rid of my sin, which, like a terrible load, was weighing me down, it seemed to me, to eternal death.

I tried in vain to get some help from the law; it only aggravated my guilt, and I was well nigh despair. At last Jesus showed me this promise: "Though your sins be as scarlet, they shall be as white as snow; though they be red like crimson, they shall be as wool." Here was hope for me. I got some light, but was conscious of no joy. I had lost my burden, and never found it again as it then troubled me. I have been in darkness, in doubts, in distress of mind, but never has that sense of just condemnation for my sin returned.

I did not immediately confess Christ, as there was no revival, and none to encourage me. When I did (which was nearly two years after), I had joy and peace such as I never before had known. When I was sixteen, I tremblingly related my Christian experience, and was baptized upon a profession of faith in Christ. For a while I lived near to Christ, but temptation came, and I yielded. Soon I repented, confessed my sin to God, and was accepted of him. I did not, in the opinion of the church, backslide; for I was very punctual in attendance upon all the outward forms of religion, and especially the meetings of the church. Yet, for five or six years, I lived in the *endurance*, rather than the *enjoyment* of religion, except in seasons of revival, when it was pleasant to wait on God, and " I was glad when they said unto me, Come, let us go up to the house of the Lord." When these seasons were past I soon lost my delight in obedience, yet dared not relinquish my profession of religion, or practice of its duties.

Once, while in this state, I took up a little work on holiness, by what author I do not now remember. This carried conviction to my mind that I was not living up to my privilege as a Christian. I asked some professors of religion about the state of grace described in the book. Some said it was attainable, while others declared that it was fanaticism to believe such a thing, and earnestly tried to prejudice my mind against the doctrine, which was represented to me to be a dangerous error. I could not, however, but wish in my heart that it was true. To me there was a great beauty in holiness of heart and life; and, although I did not embrace the doctrine, but took strong grounds against it, yet I grew less and less satisfied with my way of living. I felt the need of a deeper work of grace, but could not tell what was the hindering cause.

It seems strange to me now that I was so blind. Yet I did, in spite of all, go on in the old way, and tasted again the cup of sin, and tried to find comfort in vanity and folly. I wonder the church did not see it; but no one reproved me, if they did. I did not stop praying or attending the means of grace; but I lived very, *very* far from my Saviour.

God put his hand upon me—I felt it. My pleasures, which had deluded me, were turned to gall; I was terribly afflicted with melancholy. I tried very hard to get rid of my trouble, which was known to none but God and my own soul. I prayed, but found no relief—no light. I became alarmed, and cried to God in anguish. Finally I was relieved from my peculiar trouble. I never knew till very lately the meaning of it. I can now see that God was disciplining me, and I thank him for it.

I was then nearly twenty-one years of age. I looked out upon life with new eyes. What was I to do? Many schemes flashed upon my mind. Involuntarily the question came: "Can you honor God in this course?" I never saw, before, the necessity of seeking to know God's will in all things. I saw plainly that I had rashly tried to go alone. I had been a wayward child. Oh, that I could find his favor again! I would submit to him in all things. It was a long, severe struggle to get all on the altar; but, by the help of God, I made the consecration. If I ever felt the power of God upon me, it was then.

I saw souls perishing. I must work for them. I was teaching; I began to labor for the conversion of my scholars, and God helped me. I have since seen some glorious results of that winter's labor. The winter of '57 and '58 is one full of blessed recollections.

But I was not as fully consecrated as I supposed—or, if I was, I took back a part of the price—for, when I saw it my duty to preach, I refused. Darkness, like that of midnight, clouded my soul, till I yielded that point. Again I felt the approving smile of my Saviour, and again had a burden for souls. God was with me, and I loved the work. Here, however, I began to see my own weakness as I never had seen it before. When I had a *good time*, I was elated; and when I failed, I was cast down. My conscience told me that was *pride—vain pride*. Oh, how many sorrowful hours it has cost me; hours of bitter anguish. I prayed for victory; I got it for the time, but still it lived —lived to be my *spiritual bane*.

I loved to preach about the glory and power of Jesus as a Saviour. My heart would glow with rapture for a while when pursuing this theme, when suddenly the thought came: "If there is so much power in Christ, why is it not more effectual on your heart? Why is not all this a *living reality to you?*" I was troubled continually with these thoughts whenever I tried to speak on my favorite theme, "the love of Jesus." I examined myself, and tried to find the difficulty. Conscience said my heart was not right. I tried to consecrate myself anew, hoping that I should in that way get right. I thought I had all on the altar; I was willing to be anything or nothing, only that God would carry on his work. We were praying for a revival. I had a great burden for souls—could trust in God for salvation for perishing sinners, but there was a void in my own soul. I talked with brethren in the ministry about my feelings. One exhorted me to stop thinking about myself and *work* more for sinners. I thought this advice strange, for I was at *work* as hard then as my feeble body would allow, for the salvation of others. I saw he did not understand my case. I was not afraid of going to hell—I was longing to be pure in heart. I had thought much of the doctrine of entire sanctification, and had felt it my duty to denounce the doctrine as a dangerous error. I was encouraged to do this by many of my brethren in the ministry, and verily thought I ought to do it. Yet, while I was in this state of mind, I often, in secret, found myself praying that God would cleanse me from all sin. Once, while leading in public prayer during the revival, I felt constrained to pray for us as a church, that we might be entirely sanctified; but, before my words uttered the thought of my heart, I paused, and in order to be consistent, prayed that "God would make us just as good Christians as it *was possible for us to be in this life.*"

The work went on, but, as it deepened, I saw more and more the sinfulness that lingered in my heart. Pride, envy, and selfishness never looked so heinous before. How could I honor God with all these things about me? I was in distress. I asked the prayers of my brethren in a prayer-meeting. I told them I was seeking what I termed a deeper work of grace. They did not seem to understand what I meant. Soon after, a Methodist lady, an excellent sister in Christ, suggested to me that I was a seeker not only after a deeper work of grace, but what their church call *entire sanctification*. My heart said that was true. My pride was offended; I began to see where I was; that I did long to be entirely cleansed from sin, but had been too proud to acknowledge the fact. It may have been simple prejudice, but I think my besetting sin had much to do with it. I asked God to show me the light clearly on this question, and I would follow it whatever the consequences might be.

I prayed and searched the Bible; I saw clearly that God loved holiness—he required it. "Be ye holy, for I am holy." The apostle Paul prayed for his brethren that they might be "sanctified wholly." That was just what I needed. Would God require us to be anything that we could not become by his grace? Would the apostle pray for that which could not be granted, namely, the sanctification and preservation of a Christian in a state of *blamelessness* before God?

I found all my former prejudices fast leaving me, for I was in a terrible strait, and any way out, that God would approve, was acceptable. It was life or death with me. If sanctification was only accomplished at death, and I must continually dishonor God by sin till that time, I hoped that life would be short; but, if there was any power that could cleanse me from all unrighteousness, I was ready to accept it. If received at all, it must be through Christ: that was plain. I turned to Ephesians and read, "Unto him who is able to do exceeding abundantly above all that we ask or think, according to the power that worketh in us," etc. Ah, I could *think*, I could *ask* for full salvation! *He* was "*able*" to do just what I needed to have done, just what I desired most of all to be done. "Do what thou wilt with me, come what will, persecutions, anguish of body, loss of all things, even death, only cleanse from all sin, and make me holy, so that I may glorify thee in all I do," was my prayer. But my anxiety and longing only increased. I saw the prize full in view, attainable almost, yet I could not call it mine. I sought counsel and advice from the sister above named. She told me to *believe*. I tried, but could not fully; there was a chasm I could not bridge. I called in a brother who enjoyed this blessing; he went with me into my study; I told him I had set apart that day to seek God by fasting and prayer for *full* salvation. He showed me that it was entirely of grace, and not by our work; that we must cast ourselves on Christ, and *trust* him. I saw where I was, viz.: 1. I desired this grace. 2. I believed that God was able to bestow it. 3. That God was *willing* to bestow it upon all that *believe.* But would he grant *me* this grace now? Could I believe now? Again the text, "Unto him that is able to do exceeding abundantly above all we ask or think," came to my mind, as if it was written for me. We bowed in prayer together. My soul could rest on God's word somewhat. I told the Lord all about my doubts that I had had, and asked him if he was well pleased with my seeking this grace, to give me the witness of his Spirit. It came: I felt then I could rest upon the precious promises of the word, and while I was meditating upon the wondrous love of God, "Or ever I was aware, my soul made me like the chariots of Aminadab."

I feel it most blessed to be able "to reckon myself dead indeed unto sin, and alive unto God through our Lord Jesus Christ." I have been greatly strengthened in testifying to the power of Jesus' blood to cleanse from all sin. I have as yet met with no persecution, but I dare not pray God to keep me from it. I want no will of my own aside from his will in all things. I have found a number who are seeking this grace in my own congregation, and in the vicinity, belonging to other societies. May God lead them in a plain path, and bring them out into gospel liberty. I ascribe *all the glory* to God, Father, Son, and Holy Ghost, for salvation. And now, in the light of six years' experience, I can say that the blessed effects of the grace then received have been with me ever since. Imperfections have marred my life's history, but I have the abiding assurance that Jesus is a perfect Saviour, and now, as then, "Able to do exceeding abundantly above all we ask or think." But I am so conscious of my own unworthiness and weakness that I feel it will be an amazing wonder of grace if I am ever permitted to enter heaven.

EXPERIENCE OF MRS. E. P. G.

THIRTY-TWO years ago, on my eighteenth birthday, I put on Christ in baptism, and through all these years have been trying to follow him; but too much of the time, like Peter, "afar off," alternately hoping and fearing, and joying and sorrowing. This part of my experience will be understood without my particularly repeating it. Two years ago last April I first saw a copy of the "Beauty of Holiness." I read it, and was charmed with its spirit, although my prejudices arose against the doctrine it so beautifully advocated. I turned to the "law and testimony" to see whether these things were so, and the more I read and prayed the clearer seemed the conviction of a "more excellent way." I soon began to long to walk in this way, "the King's highway of holiness," but did not see how I, with my poor, treacherous, faithless heart, could dare claim the blessing of sanctification as mine. At times it seemed to be within my reach, and I felt, oh, how eager to grasp it; but how dare I think or say that one so full of imperfections as I was could be cleansed from sin, and serve God with a pure heart?

Again, I would read the beautiful promises and exhortations touching the doctrine of holiness, and be so charmed with the view of the Christian life, it would seem as though I could not wait any longer without the assurance that my soul was freed from the bondage of corruption.

I well remember one night, when kneeling to pray, before retiring, I felt that if God would answer that prayer with a sense of his presence, I would believe. Well, while praying it seemed as though some one whispered in my ear: "Cry out and shout, thou inhabitant of Zion, for great is the Holy One of Israel in the midst of thee." I could not sleep, after retiring, for the words, "Cry out and shout," kept sounding in my ear till I felt constrained to cry out, "Glory be to God." I did not at once realize that God did indeed reveal himself to me, when the Spirit said, "Great is the Holy One of Israel in *the midst of thee.*" Ah, me! I wonder that the blessed Spirit did not leave me then, because I still doubted his word. I was waiting for the evidence—*the feeling*—that I was sanctified, before I could *believe;* but that is not the way. "*Believe*, and be saved."

It was some two months after this—I think, on the 27th of October, while about my morning work—that I was again arrested with the passage: "How long halt ye between two opinions? If the Lord be God, serve him." I felt I had no right to move another step till I fully believed in God, and then and there I knelt and surrendered *myself all* to God, in a new and living covenant. The language of my soul was:

"Just as I am, without one plea,
But that thy blood was shed for me,
And that thou bidd'st me come to thee,
O Lamb of God, I come."

And—praise his name—he received me just as he said he would, and filled me with joy and peace. I have learned the meaning of the words: "Thou wilt keep him in perfect peace whose mind is stayed on thee, because he trusteth in thee."

I have been led through many severe trials during the past year, but God has counselled me to buy of him "gold *tried* in the *fire*, that I may be rich," and—all glory be to his name—I have a little of *that* bank-stock, and from time to time it is increased with interest. And he has given me "white raiment, that I may be clothed," and he has "delivered me out of the hands of my enemies, that I might serve him without fear, in holiness and righteousness before him all the days of my life." Although I have had some hours when—walking by sight—the future of earth has looked dark and cheerless, yet faith has gained the victory; and I thank God, who giveth me the conquest over sin, and fear, and unbelief.

EXPERIENCE OF REV. J. J. M.,

A PASTOR IN MASSACHUSETTS.

THE first eighteen years of my life were passed without an evangelical conviction of sin. There were years of instruction at home and in the house of God, so that the time when I first heard of Christ, or when I first received many of the truths of the gospel is not remembered. Then there came a sense of sin and of danger, which was not heeded, and shortly wore away. A year later, and one Sabbath a few words in a sermon, conveying a statistical fact, bearing upon the operations of grace, drew my attention. Two days after this, having decided to seek God, I knelt and uttered my first prayer, and God answered it with salvation. From the time my new-born faith recognized itself, which was only a few hours after that first prayer, I have never had a serious doubt of my acceptance in Christ. For nine years I have reason to believe my brethren regarded me as a consistent and active Christian. While sincerely believing in Christ, and desiring in some degree to do his will, and to win souls, there was much in my heart which was not Christlike. I now see that, though the Holy Spirit began to lead me, I soon adopted the standards of Christian life, which were held among the more active members of the church, and thus, only for a short time, continued wholly to follow the Lord. Much in my heart and life was not submitted to Christ. My zeal in his service was often self-sustained, and my works self-originated.

Very early in my experience my attention was called to the subject of a holy life, and I became convinced, from the word of God, that it was his will that we should be sanctified. The only views with which I was acquainted were the Wesleyan, and those commonly held in our own churches, *i. e.*, Christians ought to become holy, but it is not possible in this world; with the latter view I was dissatisfied. The Wesleyan, for want of a better, was in some sense adopted. Sometimes I prayed about the matter, and tried to bring my soul to the place of faith, but it seemed too great work, and I would become discouraged. At length God met me with light and blessing. I had been upon my knees before him, a subdued spirit had rested upon me for days, burdens had come and wrestling for souls, the windows of heaven were being opened, and the great rain was coming upon the dry places, souls were being converted, a power rested upon the assemblies of the people, salvation had come, and my burden had lifted; I wondered if I was so soon satisfied, and if I was losing my interest.

The work went on. I was in my room, alone with God, and had thought of the wants of my own soul in my petitions, yet knew not that the Master, who was so graciously blessing in these ways, was so near with other gifts, and that he was leading my soul toward a door which no man openeth. I had risen from prayer, but the spirit of prayer was still around me. I began to write, in preparation for the approaching Sabbath, very simple truth; yet the words were borne along in my mind upon a current of glowing emotion, to which I was not accustomed. And now should I not embrace this favoring gale, which seemed sent to waft me heavenward from a long calm? Should I not *now* launch out upon God? He invited me to come. He said: "Only believe!" May I not say that he spoke to me, not through the outer, but in the inner ear?—

that he led me to the brink, not of despair, but of hope; to the place where human efforts and foundations come to an end; where the shore is bold, and the step, if it be taken Christward, will be a step off upon God into the things unseen, as though it were a leap in the dark?

Yes, he led me. I made the leap, and rested in Christ and in light. I felt at once that new grace had come, knew it not alone by outward signs, but by that spiritual revelation or intuition in which faith declares itself, or is declared by God. There were tokens accompanying, and evidences have followed, but I could even then speak that which I knew. I was not excited, in the common sense of the term, not so as to be disturbed and tossed. The emotion was rather of weight without weariness, a fulness, an incoming tide of joy and peace; yet so strong was the emotion, that my body felt and testified to its power in a manner altogether new to me. I found that I had reached a new outlook upon the Christian life. The kingdoms of this world had receded, *the kingdom* had advanced, the vision had cleared, the office of faith had been extended, the Christian life was all, no place was found for any life not Christian; the Master was calling me no longer servant, but friend.

But the gift was sent not alone for the sake of the joy. I felt that my reception and standing in the grace given included a fulfilment on my part of the gospel requirement, to be no longer my own, but Christ's in all things. As I went forth thus to follow him, the way was as narrow again as when I first entered it. There were many things I felt I ought to do which were very trying to the flesh. God tested the grace which he had given in various ways, and with seeming severity, for the tests were directed against the weak points in my nature, and where self was most strongly intrenched. My burden in these respects often seemed all I could bear, yet never in the severest trial of strength and faith did I feel to turn back. "Let me die rather than turn from thy will," was my prayer. God led me through cross-bearing in a blessed way, opening his word to my mind, and filling my heart with the sense of his love.

Especially was the truth concerning the work and guidance of the Holy Spirit made known, and I learned that it was not in the great amount of service which one might seek to do, or in the heavy crosses he might seek to bear, that God is pleased, but only in the doing of the service and the bearing of the crosses which he assigns; that it was our privilege to know and obey his will in our daily life, for there began to appear, not only in the letters, but written in my heart, the blessed words: "He calleth his own sheep by name and leadeth them out; he goeth before them, and the sheep follow him, for they know his voice."

The years which have followed have been years of grace, in which there have been conscious intercourse with God, and guidance of the Spirit, and definitions of experience such as I never knew before. My Father is my friend. He gives himself for me to lean upon. Lacking wisdom, I go to him and ask concerning little as well as larger things. He is never upon a journey, never far off, he always hears. The way is dark or it is light, but all alike to him. If things agree with my natural inclinations or wisdom, it is pleasant; if not, it is still sweet to feel that his way is best, and that he will neither send, nor allow to come, aught which shall be evil in the end. My soul has not to bear the burdens of the world, nor the care of to-morrow, but only to walk on with Christ, its prayer being the answering back to the words which Jesus speaks, and to the love he breathes; its work, to believe on him, and to do whatsoever he saith. In this walk there is yet much of weakness on my part.

Sanctified in the sense of full acceptance in Christ, I feel I am; but some of the revelations of self—of my heart and its wants, and the greatness of the work to be accomplished—would have been discouraging if they had not been preceded by faith, which enabled me to bear the sight, knowing whose hand lifted the vail. Perfection and glory are far, and yet near; near in God's time. May his time be mine evermore!

EXPERIENCE OF MRS. L. J. H.

SO far as my conversion is concerned, I have no doubt. The change was very great and decided; from feelings of indescribable agony, on account of sin, to perfect peace and joy. But never was I satisfied with my attainments in the divine life. I was always longing for a

> "Closer walk with God,
> A higher, holier frame,"

and would most earnestly have sought for all my heart desired had I supposed it possible for me to attain to it; but I used to think that none but ministers and their wives, or missionaries, could live so as to enjoy so rich an experience as some enjoyed, of whom I had read; and I often wished it could have been my happy privilege to be a missionary. I thought that they were rather to be envied than pitied. And while I knew I could be very much more active in the cause of my Master than I had been, or was, still the fear of being called "overmuch righteous," or of making myself too conspicuous, kept me back in what I knew would be thought my proper place; and I seldom dared to express all that was in my heart, lest others might suppose that I was trying to make them think me better than I really was, and *that* I always shrank from.

But some five years ago there was a revival in the place where I then resided, and my dear pastor's wife met with a very great change in her feelings, at which we were all surprised, and wondered. But some thought it would pass away with the revival interest, and took but little notice of it. But it seemed to me to be just what I had been longing for, and I watched her closely as time passed on, but could see no change. Her interest in religion remained the same after the meetings became dull, as before.

I soon left there, on a visit to N., and while speaking of her experience to a friend, she said to me: "I should think she enjoyed the 'higher Christian life!'" and asked if I had ever seen the book by that title. I said no; but wished I could, as I had never heard of it before. I had never so much as heard that there was such an experience as the *higher life;* and I was exceedingly anxious to obtain the book as soon as possible, that I might learn how this prize could be reached.

I soon returned to the dear church with which I was united, and found my pastor's wife had the book, and was very anxious I should read it, and also that I should seek with all my heart for the sweet peace which she enjoyed; and more than that, for the "gift of the Holy Spirit." In reading that book I found that it was possible for persons in humble life to have the same rich blessing if they desired and would seek earnestly for it. I resolved I would make it my daily prayer and business to seek and obtain all that God had in store for me, and for some three months I was almost continually breathing after the precious gift. I read, wept, and prayed daily, and for two weeks hourly; but I was seeking it in my own way; I wanted to feel just as my dear sister did, and not until I was willing that God should do all the work in his own time and way did I find relief.

In great distress I bowed before him and gave myself up, as I did at first, unreservedly and wholly. He removed my burden and comforted my heart, but did not then grant me his special presence. But after a few hours of reading and meditation I again sought the divine blessing in humble prayer, and my precious Saviour met me there. Oh! blessed season of communion with my best-beloved! How I love to live it over and over again!

I found nearer access to the mercy-seat than ever before. My Saviour never seemed so near and so precious as there and then. I was lifted above the world, and realized, as never before, the meaning of these words: "They shall mount up with wings as eagles!"

My heart was so filled with the love of Christ, it seemed to me that I could feel it a privilege to suffer anything, or even die for him, if I could only have his blessed presence. But I can not tell how I felt as I would like to. Suffice it to say that, although I thought I was as happy as I could be when first converted, I knew nothing of the happiness I at this time experienced; and I have felt different ever since, as my faith in Christ has been stronger, and I have been able to take him as my complete sanctification.

EXPERIENCE OF REV. D. B. GUNN,

PASTOR IN ILLINOIS.

BEING favored with pious instructors, I was blessed with very early religious impressions. I can recollect, when very young, of trying to preach, and thinking I must be employed in leading sinners to Christ, and doing good generally. Although I was a rude and petulant boy, I soon learned that I was a sinner against God, and must be converted, or I could not be instrumental in saving others, nor even be saved myself. Notwithstanding, years passed away, and I was a rebellious sinner, and a Christless child. But God, who is rich in mercy, and sovereign in power, did not purpose that I should always be indifferent to my soul's best interests; for, when about nine years old, I was awakened to a sense of my lost and ruined condition. Being one evening at a prayer-meeting, I was quite deeply affected, and, at the close of the meeting, the state of my mind becoming known, several prayers were offered in my behalf, and suitable instruction was imparted, during which my sorrows ceased and my tears were dried. I could neither mourn nor weep, and had no idea that I had experienced a spiritual change. I supposed my interest was abating—that my convictions were giving way to indifference, and thought myself very ungrateful for the interest felt and the effort made in my behalf. Eagerly did I strive for conviction and tears, but all in vain; nor did I explain what the state of my mind was. But thereafter, though a child, and fond of childish sports, I was a changed person, and used to enjoy many melting seasons of communion with Jesus. The barn, the field, the wood, and my own chamber, were places where I was wont to resort, and unburden my soul in prayer.

After a few years my heart became very wayward, and for a long time, so far as I can recollect, I seldom or never prayed. I usually banished religious impressions from my mind, and at times was quite wicked.

When fifteen years old, the Lord, in great mercy, began to trouble my conscience, and for some months I was more or less concerned about my soul. In my mind a struggle was going on; while worldly pleasures presented their charms and called loudly for my attention, I was convicted of my sins and convinced of my duty, and thus, for a time, I "halted between two opinions." But what Jehovah undertakes, he will accomplish. A brother living away from home was about that time redeemed from sin by the blood of Christ. The Holy Spirit came home with him, and by his faithful efforts led me to decide that, by the help of the Lord, I would love and serve the Saviour. Soon after my mind was fully fixed to be a follower of Christ, I found several others were like-minded, and they soon began to rejoice, while I remained uncomforted, and, as I supposed, unsaved. This greatly surprised me, and at times I was very near guilty of charging my heavenly Father with injustice, for leaving me to mourn and wander in darkness. Ere long, however, my sense of condemnation was gone, and, fearing I was falling back, the burden of my prayer was: "Oh, for my load of guilt once more, and it shall not go until I *know* that I am a Christian." At length, one bright Lord's-day morning, I was led by the Spirit to trust that God, for Christ's sake, had forgiven my sins; and then, for the first time in my life, I began to hope I was a child of God.

The service of God now became my delight, and

greatly did I enjoy the Christian communion with which I was favored. My poor gifts were generally improved where opportunity presented, and usually blessings were bestowed upon me when I engaged in the Lord's work. For some time I enjoyed a pretty clear evidence of my adoption, a tolerable degree of confidence in Christ, and had no very serious obstacles to overcome, so that the Christian life was altogether inviting; but with the lapse of time, when the love of the church had waxed cold, my course became somewhat vacillating, and my life conformed to the world, and my faith, which had never been marked by peculiar strength, became quite weak, and at times seemed all changed to unbelief. Being young, and naturally fond of worldly pleasures, I tried to enjoy the vanities of life and the pleasures of religion at the same time; but this proved a vain hope; and when, after engaging in trifling conversation, participating in pleasure-parties, or anything else inconsistent with my Christian profession, I was smitten by an accusing conscience, and, reproved by the Holy Spirit, I was led to question whether I had ever known the power and efficacy of the grace of God. Thus were my fears multiplied, and my doubts greatly increased.

In seasons of refreshing I resolved to be thenceforth a devoted Christian, and, at times, my mind was much exercised upon giving myself to the public ministry of the Word; but all thoughts of this were soon abandoned, and I contented myself with the promise of a consecrated life in a more private sphere; after which I married, and engaged in secular pursuits. But I was then more than ever tried with doubts respecting my pardon and salvation. I endeavored to keep up the form of godliness; but I experienced little peace and comfort, and often I was near being miserable. It is possible that thousands of Christ's disciples live in the same way, when God's grace is all-sufficient. Oh, that every child of God could learn the easy lesson of trusting Jesus for a full, present, and eternal salvation.

I began to search for the faith of assurance, feeling that I could not go on in such uncertainty; and, in my anxiety, I hit upon this: I went to the Lord and made a promise that, if he would make me instrumental in the conversion of one soul, I would doubt no more. By the grace of God I was soon after so used in the conversion of a hardened sinner, who had seemed given over by the Spirit, that I could not doubt my instrumentality in the work of his salvation. After this I experienced no trouble about my hope for a long time; and, in obedience to the evident call of the Holy Spirit, I soon commenced to preach Christ and him crucified. Well did I love the glorious work, making a fuller consecration of myself to Christ than I had ever done before.

I was ordained and settled as pastor, and the blessing of God, to some extent, rested upon my labors. Saints were quickened and sinners converted, but still there was an evident defect in my religious experience. A deeper-toned piety, a more entire consecration, and an overcoming faith in Jesus as my perfect Saviour, were my greatest desires.

While my mind was filled with these longings, a friend put into my hands a book, entitled "The Higher Christian Life," by Rev. W. E. Boardman, which I read with great interest and profit. I seemed to find here just the instruction I needed, and I expected soon to be in the enjoyment of the "higher life," and live by faith in the Son of God. But weeks, and months, and years passed, and I was not realizing what I had anticipated, nor did I seem to be getting any nearer to it; on the contrary, I became more unbelieving, and doubts of my adoption returned to trouble me more than ever.

When I had become somewhat indifferent about this matter, the Lord called my attention to it anew through the correspondence of my dear brother, who had also become a laborer in the gospel ministry, and who has now for more than seven years been enjoying the fulness of Christ by a confiding trust. Once more I resolved fully to believe in the Saviour, and yield the fruits of a conquering faith in an entirely sanctified life. But the experience of the next two years of my life I hope never to have repeated. I could do very little rejoicing in the Lord, and his service was not attended with much delight. I resolved, and re-resolved, but resolutions are poor substitutes for the fulness of the love of Christ. I could seldom preach to my satisfaction, and when I did, I fear it resulted more in vainglory than in honor to Christ. Sometimes I almost resolved never to preach again until my own experience was richer in the grace and love of God. And my trouble was not all about myself: the church would not come up to my ideas of duty, which greatly fretted me; and I coaxed, and teased, and scolded, but all to no purpose. I preached a high standard of piety, but it was all in vain; and I at length determined to refrain from preaching so much above my own experience.

I next resigned my pastoral charge, and then set myself anew to the work of obtaining that which my soul longed for. After a few weeks, during which no perceptible advance was made, it was my happy privilege to spend a week with my brother above alluded to. I went to his residence with the impression that there was a rich blessing in store for me, and I must secure it before the week expired. But day after day passed, and I was still the same seeking, unsatisfied one, until I began to fear that I must go away as I came. Many seasons of prayer had been observed with special reference to my case, and earnest had been the pleadings of trusting Christian friends, and I had prayed, hoping, at times almost believing, that the gift would be granted, until I began to say, "Not for me."

At my brother's proposal we visited a pious, aged couple, who had enjoyed the blessing of sanctification a long time, where, after exchanging salutations and expressing our feelings and hopes, we bowed to pray. I was the only subject; my case was the whole burden of prayer; and, thanks be to God, we did not rise from our knees until that long captivity of my soul was at an end. From a cruel bondage to sin and Satan, I was set at liberty through faith in Jesus Christ my Lord. The love of Christ now filled my soul, and it was delightful to trust fully in him as my own perfect and glorious Saviour. And then it was so easy— only to submit all to him, and, with perfect, childlike confidence, fully believe in him. Oh, how wonderfully strange that I had not done it long before. But it was only by grace that I did it now; and well nigh had I failed of it altogether; for, even while we were praying, the temptation of Satan came so strongly upon me that I was on the point of concluding the blessing would never be mine, and that I must go away and live as I had done. But such was not God's purpose; Jesus came near, and still nearer; he entered my heart; he filled it; and oh, such a fulness! It is not in my power to describe it—exceeding anything I had ever experienced before: "Christ in me, the hope of glory;" *my* Redeemer, and *my* Saviour, realized by faith as no one in a partially sanctified state could do.

By grace I now live in a higher spiritual life than formerly; whether it be called "perfect love," "sanctification," "the fulness of Christ," "holiness," or "the faith of full assurance," matters not. It is the experience, and not the name that is of most importance. And I wish that every Christian would fully trust in Christ, live a holy life, and continually praise God.

I have long loved the service of God, but it is now *so delightful*—and preaching Christ, and him crucified, is now a different work to me. In fact, my whole life seems new; there is a new standpoint from which to look, new light with which to see, nearer relations, and stronger ties. Jesus is more precious, all his people more beloved, and eternal things more vividly realized. Now, all goes on smoothly; no need of chafing or fretting; everything is quiet, peaceful, joyous. This change has been effected by the power of God, and is the greatest of my whole life. God grant that now I may grow every day in holiness and wisdom, until my work is done, and I am welcomed home.

EXPERIENCE OF MRS. S. S.

I DO not remember the time when my heart was not susceptible to divine impressions. I always had a peculiar love and respect for the people of God, and especially for the ministers, whom I used to hear preach, from time to time, in the Episcopal church—for it was that denomination in which I was brought up. But God in his mercy more effectually called me, by his Holy Spirit, when I was about seventeen years old. I felt very much convicted, and thought, by being confirmed and becoming a full member of the church, I should find peace of mind, and receive pardon for my sins. Acting on these and similar convictions, I received confirmation, and became a member of the church. But I was not converted, neither did I know what conversion or change of heart meant; nor did that peace of mind come for which I was so anxious. Year after year passed away, and that aching void remained within; I was still unsatisfied. But the words of this hymn kept coming to me:

> "God moves in a mysterious way
> His wonders to perform."

Oftentimes I was very much troubled and cast down. I used to wonder if there ever was so great a sinner as I. I used to look around and see others enjoying themselves, and all seemed to go well with them, while my plans and purposes were frustrated. I would then go to some place of amusement, and try to stifle conviction, but that experiment would leave its bitter sting in my troubled soul.

All this time I was living as a professed member of the Episcopal church. But when I was about thirty-four years old, through the instrumentality of a good man, a devoted member of the Methodist denomination, I was led to a greater thoughtfulness, to deeper convictions, which resulted in the salvation of my soul. I sought the Saviour in all the means of grace, such as studying his word, and our excellent hymns, and also in private prayer. In the evening of the day on which I had been conversing with this Christian, there was a prayer-meeting, and the inquirers were invited to come forward for prayer. The altar was crowded with penitents, and I was among the number. After uniting in prayer for a short time, while good brothers and sisters were close by my side, praying for me, I received the witness that all my sins were forgiven. I seemed to see Jesus on the cross, as he said to me, "Daughter, thy sins, which are many, are all forgiven." From this time I went on my way rejoicing; and I could say with the poet:

> "Thou hast subdued my stubborn will,
> Hast bid my stormy heart 'be still;'
> Since Thou the 'aching void' dost fill,
> How doth my soul with rapture thrill."

Glory be to his holy name for the way in which he led me for about a year after my conversion. I felt that, being justified by faith, I had peace with God, through our Lord Jesus Christ—although, at times, beset with many temptations, and doubts and fears. I began to be remiss in my duty to God, especially in secret prayer. Attending to my family duties seemed to have taken up all my thoughts, and to have imperceptibly drawn my mind from God, and I lost that sweet sense of the Saviour's presence, which I had enjoyed; but I still retained my place in the church, and kept up the form of godliness. About this time the church that I had united with was sold, and some of the members went one way and some another. With the rest I took my letter. I then removed to Brooklyn to live, and, my husband not being willing that I should attend the class meetings, I did not unite with any church, but went in and out as a silent member. Step by step I receded, till at last the church troubled me but very little. I remained some time in this state; yet the Spirit of the Lord was striving with me all the time. I doubted, and so, through unbelief, I lost the blessing.

After this time I never cared for attending the Methodist church, though I still liked the people. My feelings leaned toward the Baptist denomination, and I said that if I ever united with any church again, I would take up my cross and be buried with Christ in baptism, for I could not see any other way so clear in the Bible for following Jesus and obeying his commands. I had believed, but had not been baptized. In the course of some months after these thoughts had been suggested to me, or, rather, had suggested themselves to me, an intimate friend of mine sent to tell me that she was going to be baptized, and invited me to go and witness the administration of the ordinance. At first I refused; but the Holy Spirit seemed to say to me, "You ought to go and see her." So, according to these promptings, I went, and, as I witnessed the scene, I thought it was a beautiful way to put on Christ by such an open profession. But I thought that I could never take up such a cross as that.

On the Tuesday following she invited me to the meeting. I told her perhaps I would go; but, before the time arrived, I had altered my mind, and sent my child to say that I could not accept the invitation. About six o'clock that night the Holy Spirit suggested the thought to me: "You may never have another opportunity." It was so impressed on me that I could not refuse, and I went. They had a good meeting. It was praying and speaking. One brother present said, "If there was any poor sinner there who wanted to be prayed for, let him manifest it by rising; and if there was any poor backslider there, let him manifest it by rising also." I said: "That is me; but I cannot rise here, for I do believe that I am nailed to the seat." But he repeated it again, and said: "This may be your last opportunity." I said: "I cannot hold out any longer!" I rose and told them I had wandered from the fold of God, and was very anxious to come back again to my Father's house. Then the good Lord mercifully restored unto me the joys of his salvation, and I united with the Baptist church.

Having wandered once, I was afraid that I should again. But I went often to Jesus and asked Him to lead and guide me into *all* truth. I at once made up my mind that I would work for Jesus. I was very desirous to know what my calling was. The Spirit soon impressed upon me that I should begin at home first. I did so. I began to pray for my husband. I soon saw the Lord was blessing my labors. I can now truly say he was dead in trespasses and sin, but is now made alive in righteousness, and rejoices in the Lord Jesus Christ. We both began to intercede with the Lord in behalf of my son and daughter. In the course of six months, God was graciously pleased to answer our prayers, and they, also, were rejoicing in Christ their Saviour, and were added to the church, where they still continue, and where, I trust, God's grace will enable them to continue to the end.

After my work was finished in my own home, I went out from house to house. There, also, the Lord met me, and abundantly blessed my labors, from time to time. He made me the humble instrument of bringing five more penitents to the foot of the cross. They have all been baptized in the same faith as myself. I have firm hopes that they have all been accepted of Jesus.

Soon after this, I felt my need of a deeper work of grace in my heart. I often went to God in prayer, that he would lead me in the path of holiness. Oh! how my soul thirsted and longed after true holiness! The precious promise came up before me, that we "should be filled;" and I fully believed that it was my privilege to be sanctified throughout, soul and body and spirit. Through the help of the Holy Spirit, I tried to consecrate all my redeemed powers to his service, and to lay all on the altar which sanctifies the gift; and that he received such consecration at the time, I fully believe, for I had the witness thereof within me. My earnest desires and prayers were that I might receive the full baptism of the Holy Ghost, to fit me to live and be useful in my family and the church of God. After this I had no fear as I went from one to another to speak the words the Holy Spirit put into my mouth; for I felt that it was not me, but the Spirit of God that spoke within me. Oh! I felt that it was indeed heaven upon earth to have such liberty—such freedom, after having been bound so long.

After a time, the full tide of my joys subsided, and I settled down into a sweet, solemn calm. I felt that I was the least of all the disciples of Jesus; that I wanted to sit at his feet and learn of him. Soon after this I had new crosses to take up, and more trials and severe temptations since receiving that blessing than I ever experienced before, and felt that I could not have borne up under them without this grace. But Jesus strengthened me to endure. I am now trying to do all the known will of God. I have not felt anything in my heart contrary to his love. Since I commenced writing this, I have felt strengthened to believe, and to-day feel I will trust and not be afraid; and, though he slay me, yet will I trust in him. I believe I will overcome by the blood of the Lamb and the word of my testimony.

Being led by the Holy Spirit to let my light shine, I was called upon to give my experience. As I found there were many contending against this great doctrine of holiness, I felt the more compelled to testify to its truth, as it was through the guidance of the Holy Spirit alone that I was led to embrace the great truths which that doctrine contains. Never having heard it preached from the pulpit, it was not, therefore, from the teachings of men that I was led to believe in that great work of the Divine Spirit in the heart of the believer; but it was from my own blessed experience of what that Spirit had wrought within myself. It is written, "Be ye holy, for I am holy;" for "without holiness no man shall see the Lord." Our Saviour himself says, "Be ye perfect, as your Father in heaven is perfect." St. Paul also teaches this great doctrine so plainly, that I wonder very much it is not accepted more generally. And now if any of the readers of this experience have hitherto been in doubt regarding this work of the Spirit, I trust the perusal of these lines may help to dispel the clouds which may have gathered on their understanding:

> "I take thee, precious Jesus,
>   My portion hence to be,
> All earthly things forsaking,
>   To fully follow thee.
>
> 'Tis true the way is thorny,
>   And strewn with many a cross;
> But these I gladly welcome,
>   And reckon all things loss."

EXPERIENCE OF R. B. ANDREWS,

PASTOR IN MAINE.

I OBTAINED my first knowledge of universal depravity when but five years of age. Then my father used to return nightly from his shop, and sit down and weep bitterly. I asked my mother why he wept. She replied: "He is afraid he shall die in his sins." This made an ineffaceable impression upon my tender mind, and cast a shadow across my infant pathway. I was seriously impressed with the thought that I was a sinner, with all mankind. At eight years of age I was again deeply impressed, and began to pray, and continued to do so until I was twelve. From that time until I was twenty-two I made no penitent prayers. Eight years of wasted life were spent in the belief and pertinacious defence of Universalism. So firmly was I fixed in the faith, that I commenced a course of study, with the secret intention, at some future day, of preaching this strange doctrine.

About this time my health failed, and I was obliged to relinquish my studies. In this state of physical debility, I found myself diseased morally, from the soles of my feet to the crown of my head; and, just when I needed it most, my universal panacea failed. It was a broken reed to lean on. But God's free grace rescued me, and my sorrows were turned into rejoicing. I took the Bible as my instructor, and found it sufficient. The battle between my old prejudices and the Bible was short, sharp, and decisive, and the Bible became my palladium against future error. Of course, I came out what is called a Baptist. I longed to get out of sight and hearing of the world for once, and by the grace of God I made a pilgrimage to old Hebron church as a spiritual home. It became my city of refuge.

On the 11th of August, 18—, I was buried with Christ in baptism. For eighteen months after this memorable event, my life was one of lights and shades, but I was not satisfied with such an experience, and as a Bible Christian, or rather with the Bible for my guide, I could not be content with my spiritual status. I was not up to the Bible standard. My brethren comforted me (?) with the assurance that this was the *believer's lot*. This alternating between doubt and assurance was considered the height of Christian attainment! I could not believe this with my Bible in my hand, and drew conclusions from its statements of character and doctrine.

I attended, in 1848, the Empire camp-meeting, and there learned the blessed way of holiness. I bless God that he ever sent Charles Nichols to the State of Maine. He was a Congregationalist brother of Boston. Through his instrumentality I was enabled to enter into perfect rest. My consecration was most complete. My back was turned upon the world as much as if I had been one of the eight that entered the ark. That was a glorious hour to me. My little idols went to the moles and the bats. I was an inveterate tobacco smoker. This I abandoned; I stripped my person of everything that savored of the world. I could not have felt worse had I buried my last earthly friend, and sacrificed my last dollar. But, blessed be God, he took all, and restored all again that I could desire. Yea, more; three days after this stripping-time, God endued me with power, and now my joy was full.

Nine years of experience in this way have only confirmed my hopes and made assurance doubly sure; and, whatever my allotments, I have always been able to say, "It is best; let Him do as it seemeth good." Both rod and staff have comforted me, and God has set a hedge about me. Sometimes I come up to it, and sometimes I am scarred with the thorn and thistle to remind me more forcibly of my God-drawn boundaries. Whatever comes I will count it *all* joy, and wait for God to make it so to me. I have not been disappointed for nine years. He cannot be, whose law is God's will. I now rest through faith in the atoning blood.

Eight years I have been laboring to spread this glorious salvation, and, to God be all the praise, the vintage has overrun. Many have been saved and many sanctified. Through evil and good report I have held up this mountain standard as promulgated and expounded by our Saviour on the holy heights around Jerusalem.

EXPERIENCE OF M. H.

WHEN I was in my twelfth year, the Lord spake peace to my soul, and I remember I wished that all the world could enjoy the happiness I then felt. Though I have never ceased trying to live a Christian life, yet I have had a great struggle with my unsanctified nature, which I confess has often turned me aside from walking in Christ Jesus as I received him. I always strove to overcome sin, but, by neglect of duty and unwatchfulness, failed. Although I hoped to be made holy before death, I did not know that I might enjoy this grace long before my departure. A little more than six years ago, I heard Rev. C. W. Brooks relate his experience. I wished that I could enjoy the experience of sanctification which he enjoyed, and which he received in answer to prayer. I then began to pray that I might be wholly sanctified, and the Lord heard my prayer, though it seemed as though he "sat as a refiner's fire and fuller's soap," to try me in the crucible and over the fire, and wash me thoroughly from my sin. Yet he granted me my heart's desire. All glory and honor and praise to God for this unspeakable blessing.

I rejoice in this glorious way of holiness. I feel to-day that I am wholly consecrated to Christ, and believe he will grant me grace sufficient to glorify his name all through life.

EXPERIENCE OF —. —. —.,

A BAPTIST MINISTER IN KANSAS.

I WAS brought to a knowledge of my sins and to trust in Christ for pardon and salvation through the faithful preaching of two brethren still living, in the winter of 1852. My experience at this time was clear. Although my home training was decidedly religious, I grew up a wicked boy. My life had been exceedingly selfish, though outwardly moral. From that time I date a decided change in my thinking and feeling and acting. Not self, but God became forthwith the object of my desire. I joined the Baptist church, and almost immediately began to think of preparing myself to preach the gospel. For this purpose I soon left home, and began a course of preparatory study at an academy. At this school the influence I was brought under was not the best. The world, the flesh, and the devil soon began to steal away my enjoyment of faith in Christ. I yielded. Study engrossed my time and thought. Ambition joined in the work of drawing my heart astray. Still, I maintained my place in the church, and my purpose of preaching, conscious all the while that I was making greater sacrifices than those of time and money—sacrifices of spiritual enjoyment and integrity. The fault was my own. My life there might have been a great gain to me. My faith need not have declined. Many a young man has withstood far greater temptations, with far less assistance in the right.

From this school I returned home to spend a year or so before starting for college. Although my life as a Christian thus far had been unsatisfactory to myself, I did not, so far as I can remember, doubt my conversion. My clear views of sin, and the need of faith in Christ in order to salvation, gained from the pious instructions of a mother who is now cold in death, kept me from being led away by my emotions, and so joining the church without any experience of forgiveness and justification.

During this earlier part of my religious life, while I was sometimes led astray and indulged in sin, I did no sooner indulge in it than I hated myself for so doing. I often prayed to be so completely given up to Christ that I might not violate my conscience so often, and suffer such deep self-loathing. The radical trouble with me was a latent belief that such frequent strayings and pungent repentings were the inevitable lot of all Christians. And yet, as I read my Bible I wondered if the rich experiences of early saints could not be repeated in the lives of modern Christians.

When I left home to attend college, I tried to renew my consecration to Christ and his cause. The influences that surrounded me at college were more favorable in many respects than those at the academy. Still, my life fell far short of what I knew it ought to be; but, by comparing my course with that of many who, like myself, were studying for the ministry, I rested satisfied with the belief that I was no worse than they, and that, when I once completed my collegiate studies, I would lead a more devoted life. For I knew I never could accomplish much good as a minister unless I had a deeper experience of divine grace. And yet I shrank from a personal scrutiny of my heart and a thorough readjustment of my life in the sight of God; that was to be an after-work. And so I drifted along through six years of study at the college. Not a day passed, as it seems to me now, without more of heart-condemnation than approval.

From college I went to the theological seminary. Here, too, I am ashamed to confess it, my mind was more delighted with study than my heart was with piety. I did not live right—far from it: and yet, without unjustly condemning others, few of my acquaintances in the seminary condemned me by their holy living. The standard of piety at these "schools of the prophets," is no higher, so far as I know and can learn, than at colleges. Study and scholarship are as exclusively pursued and eagerly sought after here as at any other schools. The fault is the fault of the individual students. The advantages are perverted too often.

Through the seminary course I looked forward to the ministry, with its sacred duties, as the healing-time of my soul-troubles. Yet, upon the whole, I think I made some little progress in spirituality. I think I was looked upon by my classmates and others as up to the average in point of piety.

I left the theological seminary, and proposed myself for ordination as the pastor-elect of a church. The solemn hour of the formal setting apart to the life-work of preaching Jesus I tried to improve to my soul's good. I endeavored to make it all it ought to be—an occasion of dedicating my soul to God. The hour came and went, and yet my desires were not realized. I was still dreadfully conscious of my inner deficiency. Sometimes the duties of the ministry were quite full of enjoyment to me. Again, I engaged in them officially, and not from pure love of them.

Thus things passed on for nearly three years, when God granted me such a view of my heart and of my need as a believer in Christ that I was brought to cry out: "Give me, O God, a baptism of the Holy Ghost, or I cannot preach again." Then came the fiercest struggle of my life. It was no less than a personal encounter with the unseen powers of darkness. A thick darkness fell upon my soul. Spiritual torpor, next to impossible to be shaken off, nearly paralyzed my energies. It was a terrible day, a day well-nigh of despair. Fearful doubts entered my mind. I could not be a Christian at all. This lethargy, this darkness could not certainly be the portion of a true Christian. The devil seemed very near to me. He was determined to keep me from going forward. I went again and again to my closet, till at last it seemed mockery for me to attempt to pray. With a solemn resolution that I would settle the point of my conversion or Christianity, I entered my room, determined not to leave it till I could say that I knew at least that I was a Christian. This text came to my mind: "By this we know that we have passed from death unto life, because we love the brethren." I regarded it as an answer to prayer. It came with satisfaction to my heart. I shall always thank the Lord for that passage of Scripture. Still, this was simply the removal of a doubt. It was bringing me back to where I was before. It was mostly negative. My heart yearned after some higher experiences of God and his grace. I hungered and thirsted after righteousness. I began more carefully to consecrate myself to God. I drew up a paper containing a number of different resolutions or vows of consecration, and on my knees tried by prayer to bring myself into the state of mind and heart they implied. It was a hard work, but God helped me. One by one I was able to say: "I can adopt that resolution." I continued thus in earnest prayer and solemn self-dedication till I could sign with a clear conscience the entire series. *This I look upon as the real turning-point of my experience at this time.* This was the real work it was mine to do, and on which all my subsequent and somewhat peculiar experience depended, or that without which it could not have been possible.

And this work of entire consecration is one that any Christian may and ought to make. Do not let any one begin it in order to have such and such gracious upliftings of soul; but do it because it is a perpetual duty to live in a state of entire consecration. Then God will accept the consecration, and bless the one who makes it, for Christ's sake. All real advancement in grace hinges on the consecration of the soul.

Thanks be unto God who giveth us the victory through our Lord Jesus Christ. By him I was enabled, I believe, to lay my soul and body, my education, my time, my will, my hopes, my all upon that altar, Christ, that sanctifieth the gift. Then there was a change. The blessed Jesus became mine in a fuller sense than I ever supposed it possible for me to realize in this life. From that hour simple faith took hold of him as with hooks of steel, as a Saviour able to save even unto the uttermost (utterly). How those past fifteen years of my religious life seemed to be almost in vain! And yet I did not, at that very time, doubt my conversion; neither do I now. What a glorious growth in Christ I might have enjoyed had I only thus consecrated myself years before! By-and-by, however, I was strongly tempted to believe that I had nothing more than I had previously enjoyed, and that I ought not to speak of it as anything special. So I prayed God to give me an experience that I could not doubt and that even the enemy could not gainsay. On the 8th of January, 1866, while I was conversing with a godly friend on the subject of faith, the Holy Spirit—what shall I say?—came upon me in mighty power. I could only utter his name by way of adoration for a quarter of an hour, as my friend afterwards told me. I fell upon the floor powerless, though not entirely unconscious. For more than an hour I was so filled with an awful sense of the presence of the Holy Spirit that I had to pray almost constantly that I might not shrink from what God had in store for me. I could hardly bear to hear anything spoken but the name or praises of the Third Person of the adorable Trinity.

Then came the precious Saviour and supped with me. I never saw him before as he appeared then. His love melted me till I wept aloud. During this visitation also I was lost to everything else. It was the presence of Christ and him alone. How long this continued I cannot say definitely. Perhaps it was half an hour. The tenderness, vividness, freshness and power of that blessed season of visitation (I can hardly call it anything else) from Christ, I shall never forget! It was blessedness indeed. It was not so awful as the previous experience of the presence of the Holy Spirit. It was love and sweetness in the highest sense. I loved the Saviour then with an intensity and a personal affection altogether as real and much more delightful and heavenly than any love I had ever felt or thought my soul capable of. It was being with Christ in almost more than an earthly sense.

Finally came a consciousness of the Father's love. He, too, seemed nearer, more precious and desirable than I can express. He seemed especially precious to me as my heavenly Parent. While viewing him in my soul, every other thought vanished. It was intimate communion with God as Father.

Thus it was: first, the Spirit, whom I had so nearly ignored, at least experimentally, nearly consumed me by his presence; then the Son manifested himself unto me as he does not unto the world and as he had not unto me; and finally, the

Father drew near, oh, so near, to me. It was a spiritual view of each person of the Trinity, only in the inverse order.

I wish to add that at this time I was in strong health, was not overworked, or in any way nervously excited. I was cool and collected, but greatly in earnest in the pursuit of godliness, as God enabled me to be.

I still distinguish, although it is now four years since it occurred, this experience from my conversion. It was something, let the name be what it may, wholly distinct from conversion, and something, moreover, which I believe any child of God may enjoy; perhaps not in just the same form, but practically the same. I mean, *any Christian can consecrate himself wholly to God; and if he does, God will bless him in his own good way.* The principal practical results are, a deeper and richer insight into the Word of God, greater power in preaching it, a surer sense of God's presence, a stronger hold of Christ as my eternal salvation, and a much stronger and more lively faith in the personality and presence of the Holy Spirit.

May God lead us all into the *rest of faith*, up into the higher life of peace, power, and joy in the Holy Ghost, for Jesus' sake.

EXPERIENCE OF MRS. H. A. PARKER.

ONE Monday morning, in consequence of listening to the spirit-stirring and heart-searching discourses preached in our house of worship the day previous, I became so overwhelmed with a view of my own weakness and insufficiency to do anything acceptable to God, my shortcomings and the state of my sinful heart, that I was on the verge of despair. I resorted to my place of secret communings with my Saviour, and so terrible was my grief, that, but for the assistance of divine grace, I must have yielded to the tempter, and concluded that there was no mercy for such a one as I. I laid myself before my God, and begged, and wept, and groaned, and besought him for mercy.

I said: "Dear Saviour, for the honor of thine own name and cause which I so dearly love, reveal thyself; manifest thyself anew to me, *even to me*, unworthy as I am, lest I die. Let me see thee as thou art, and lose sight of self and all else that may hinder my experience of *entire, perfect trust* in thee for all needed grace and strength. Remove this fear of condemnation and sense of guilt, and help me to rely upon thee wholly for salvation, or I am undone!" It seemed as if the Saviour said to me: "If there could have been any other way—if you could possibly have lived pure and holy enough to have merited salvation—what need of the great sacrifice of myself? What need of my having stood in your place, and expiated your guilt? What need of the shedding of my blood to wash away your sins? What need of my bearing the frown of an offended God and Judge."

I exclaimed: "It is enough! my Saviour and my Redeemer, my Sanctifier, and my Deliverer!" And then my life and myself were so completely hid in Christ, that I saw nothing, knew nothing, but Christ, and him crucified for *me*. I entirely forgot that I had any existence, any interest, separate from Jesus and his cause. My soul was lighted up with such a heavenly radiance and weight of glory, far beyond my power to describe; I became so completely swallowed up in Christ, and lost to all but him; his perfect atonement for all my sins was so real and so fully realized by simple faith.

I lost sight of self and sin, and knew not who or where I was. He in me, and I in him. "I in them and thou in me, that they may be made perfect in one." (John 17 : 23.)

How long this lasted I know not. It all might have appeared in a moment, and it might have lasted many minutes. This I know: the time, the place, and the experience will never be effaced from my memory, and I shall carry its hallowed influence through all my future life. If ever my sins, my own unworthiness, or myself, present themselves in any way to dampen my spirit, lessen my enjoyment, weaken my faith, or threaten my peace, my Saviour's words, "If there could have been any other way," are enough.

Glory be to his name! Praise and adoration and love be given to Christ my righteousness, my all in all, now and forever, for his unspeakable gift to me.

The following Scripture is exceedingly full of richness and beauty to me: "There is therefore, now, no condemnation to them who are in Christ Jesus, who walk not after the flesh, but after the Spirit, for the law of the Spirit of life in Christ Jesus has made me free from the law of sin and death. For what the law could not do, in that it was weak through the flesh, God, sending his own Son in the likeness of sinful flesh, and for sin, condemned sin in the flesh, that the righteousness of the law might be fulfilled in us who walk not after the flesh, but after the Spirit." (Rom. 8: 1-5.)

"Stand fast therefore in the liberty wherewith Christ has made us free." (Gal. 5: 1.)

"He that overcometh shall inherit all things, and I will be his God and he shall be my son. (Revelations 21: 17.)

EXPERIENCE OF W. E. NOYES,

A PASTOR IN MAINE.

ON the 17th day of March, 1857, the Lord in mercy regenerated my sinful heart. Some three days afterwards, "being justified by faith, I found peace with God, through our Lord Jesus Christ." I soon found "the flesh lusting against the spirit, and the spirit against the flesh; these were contrary the one to the other, so that I *could not do the things that I would.*" Nearly two years passed away, during which time I was constantly struggling (by *works*, though ignorantly) to overcome the "old man," yet without complete success, all the while groaning and singing:

> "When I pray, or sing, or read,
> *Sin* is mixed with *all I do.*
> You who love the Lord indeed,
> Tell me—*is it so with you?*"

Very often crying, as in the seventh chapter of Romans, "Oh, wretched man that I am, who shall deliver me?"

When I looked to my older brethren (I was then a Congregationalist), I gained no encouragement at all that I should ever be "delivered from this body of death," or the "carnal mind," until death. Then I would *pray* and *long for death to deliver me.* But when I looked to *Jesus and his gospel*, then I saw that there *was* deliverance while in health and strength, as taught in 1 Thess. 5 : 23, 24; 1 Peter, 4 : 1, 2; Romans, 6 : 2, 6, 7, and 22. Hence I determined, with the help of the Lord, that I would gain *complete victory* over carnal nature, and be *wholly the Lord's*, "wholly sanctified," or would *die in the attempt.* This determination I made known to my friends just before leaving home for the east, at the call of the Lord, to preach "the glorious gospel of the blessed God."

I left Abington, Mass., Feb. 9, 1859 (having laid my beloved wife in the tomb but a few days previous), and a few days after called on some Christian friends at Mechanic Falls, Me., on my way farther east. They invited me in to their (Baptist) conference in the afternoon, which I enjoyed very well. After the meeting closed, and all had departed but my two friends, "they took me (as Aquila and Priscilla did Apollos) and expounded unto me the way of God more perfectly." They exhorted me to believe in Jesus now for sanctification, and instructed me how to believe; not to *feel*, but **BELIEVE**.

The devil said "Methodism," the Lord said "gospel truth." The Spirit was poured upon us in mighty power, in answer to their prayers. They shouted, and "praised God with a loud voice." I groaned in darkness and unbelief, convicted powerfully, yet unsanctified, because unbelieving: "through sanctification of the Spirit and *belief of the truth*," the work must be done. I could say I *will* believe; but to say I *do* believe was the point to be gained. For two and a half hours did they fasten me there, under the power of God's word and Spirit, which was "sharper (to me then) than any two-edged sword," piercing down into my heart to its very bottom, cutting every thread and fibre that was clinging to any earthly object. Then I knew, as never before, what John the Baptist meant by the promised "baptism of fire."

At length my unbelieving and stubborn will and heart yielded all, and tremblingly did I say: "I *do* believe that Jesus cleanses me *now*, and will forever keep me holy," as promised in 1 John, 1 : 9; 1 Cor., 10 : 13, etc. We went to our place of abode, and while my two dear friends slept sweetly and soundly all night long, *resting in Jesus*, I lay awake most of the night, in a *terrible battle with Satan*, who was determined to wrest my "shield of faith" from me, and get me into trouble and doubts, telling me that I was still unsanctified and unholy, because (not having received the full witness or evidence of my acceptance) I felt no especial difference in my mind or heart. But the Lord gave me overcoming faith, and in the morning I took the New Testament and asked the Lord to give me proof of my sanctification. I opened, as the Lord directed, to the 5th chapter of Romans, and read to the last of the eighth chapter, and the doctrine of sanctification, crucifixion, and freedom in Christ from sin, never shone into my poor unworthy heart before as then, the Spirit witnessing powerfully that the long-coveted blessing and experience was mine.

Since that time I have rejoiced in a complete Saviour, sometimes enjoying more of the *power* than at other times, but always enough to "keep the *body under*, and bring it into subjection."

The dear brother who led me to Jesus for justification was Rev. A. B. Earle, the Evangelist, who holds a large place in my heart's affections. The dear brother who led me to Jesus for sanctification was Rev. R. B. Andrews (assisted by Bro. Bumpus), who is still preaching this same glorious faith, and winning many souls, and whom I hold in loving remembrance.

The Lord saves sinners and sanctifies his children through weak instrumentalities, and glory be to his name forever. Amen and Amen.

EXPERIENCE OF MRS. M. A. T.

I UNITED with the Baptist Church at the age of seventeen. I had but very little light, but hoped I was a Christian. I remained in this state about twenty-three years, when the Holy Spirit showed me I was not what a Christian should be. Through his help I sought and found Jesus precious to my poor heart. I knew, without a doubt, that Christ was my Saviour, but I found that there was inbred sin in my heart, and oh, it grieved me to think I still had sin there. I saw pride and anger (which were my darling sins), and I felt I must get rid of them.

The blessed Saviour soon led me to see that it was my privilege to be saved from all unrighteousness. I asked, how could I worship God in spirit and in truth when there was sin in my heart? Still, I did not feel that I was condemned, but felt my Father owned me as his child. I felt as I never felt before. All glory to his holy name! I was alive to God and his cause. I soon found that this doctrine of salvation from all sin was rejected by most of my brethren, but the Lord still led me on, amid all opposition. I had deep and earnest desires after God. I felt that nothing could satisfy me but to know that I was what God would have me be. I felt he would have me saved from all sin.

I attended meeting nearly every evening for several weeks, part of the time at the Baptist church, but most of the time at the Methodist meetings, they being nearer by. My desire after God increased, and one night I went to the Methodist meeting, and as soon as the minister got through preaching, he gave an opportunity for speaking. I arose and told my feelings. The minister invited all that desired the blessing of holiness to come forward for prayers. I was the first one that came forward, but soon four or five more came forward with me. We knelt for prayers. I prayed, and others prayed for me. While here, God blessed me as never before, but still I did not feel the work was done.

I went home with a heart burning with the love of God. I retired to my bed, but was so happy that I could not get to sleep for some time, but finally did, and in my sleep I dreamed that I saw a light, and I was exerting myself to reach that light. I soon awoke, my heart still burning with the love of God, but felt the work was not done yet. I still held on to God in prayer to cleanse my heart from all sin. In a few moments I felt a quiet rest; no ecstasy of joy, but all seemed calm and peaceful.

The next day I felt a more perfect resting in Jesus than I ever had before; but I soon felt I must have a *clearer* evidence that I was saved from all sin, and I began praying for the full assurance. In two or three days the witness came. I knew the blood of Jesus cleansed me from all unrighteousness. I felt it all through my soul. Praise his holy name! I rose, but soon felt like getting down to pray again, and, with an eye of faith, I saw myself at the feet of Jesus, gradually sinking into my Saviour. I was filled with God, and for almost twenty-four hours I could not ask a favor of God, for I was entirely satisfied, and

> "Drew from heaven that sweet repose
> Which none but he who feels it knows.'

Since that time, in the strength of my loving Saviour, I have endeavored to walk in all the light that God has given me. I feel that the school of Christ is a blessed school. While writing, I feel the sweet assurance that Jesus saves me from all sin, and still my cry is:

> "Nearer, my God, to thee;
> Nearer to thee."

The more I learn of my blessed Saviour, the more I see and feel that without him I am perfect weakness, perfect folly, and perfect sinfulness. Praise God for a perfect Saviour who can save to the uttermost.

EXPERIENCE OF G. F. PENTECOST,

PASTOR IN BROOKLYN, N. Y.

MY soul has been led out into a large place, and I have been brought into REST. One night in the month of August, 1865, while I was pastor in Indiana, we had a prayer-meeting, and God was with us. To me he was precious. I spoke of his goodness and love to me, and as I spoke I was filled with a weight of love and glory. I was led, in presence of the brethren, and contrary to my own purposes, to *profess* my entire consecration *to* Christ, and *confess* my entire sanctification *in* him; by which I mean,

First, that I have laid all that I have and am on the altar, and, worthless and unworthy as it all is in itself, yet, for Jesus' sake, God has accepted it from me in the name of his Son.

Second, while I feel myself a vile sinner, and unworthy of the least of God's favors, yet I feel that I am "complete in Him who is head of all principality and power;" and, while there is nothing about me that is perfect, nevertheless God sees me only through the perfection of Christ, and *counts* me as perfect, standing *in* him; and, while every moment realizing myself a sinner, and in need of pardon, he is at the right hand of God making intercession for me, and "the blood of Jesus Christ, his Son, cleanseth me from all sin."

Oh, precious thought! Christ is mine, and I am his. I am at peace—at rest. When this blessed experience was first realized, I cannot tell, as to day or hour; I only know that it is mine *now*. Neither do I base or rest it upon any feeling that I have or may have had, but I rest the whole matter of my "wisdom, righteousness, sanctification, and redemption," on God's Word, and that alone. I feel that each day I shall grow stronger in the Lord and in the power of his might. I feel much strengthened since I publicly confessed Christ as my sanctification, and I am willing to be a witness for Jesus to all who may hear or read.

EXPERIENCE OF MRS. E. W. T.,

AN AGED DISCIPLE IN ILLINOIS.

I SPENT my youthful days in Cornwall, Ct. When I was twenty-one years of age, the Lord showed me that I had sinned long enough against him, and that it was time for me to repent. I was then teaching school. In the school-room, I promised God that after I attended the Independence ball, I would be a Christian. I thought, as I was so willing to be a Christian, God would soon convert me; but I found it not so easy as many do in these days. I struggled on for many months. About the first of March, I gave up working at anything—I felt so bad. I went to several Christians, and asked them to tell me what to do. I thought if they had experienced religion, they could tell me how I could be saved.

One evening, I felt that my heart was harder than the hardest rock. My tears were dried, and I thought, if I was lost, I could not help it. I was then in meeting. While walking home, all at once these words came into my mind: "Not of yourselves; it is the gift of God." I thought they were in the English Reader. I stepped more lightly—my hard heart was gone. I thought my convictions had left me, and could not get them again. The stars seemed to shine remarkably bright. I dared look up, but I had no evidence that I was born again. As soon as I came into the house, my friends told me I was converted. I told them not to encourage me to cherish a false hope; when I was converted, I should know it for myself.

The next day I felt I needed some rest. I lay down and slept about two hours, and awoke with a feeling of despair. In a moment, I saw that I had received some light, but was not willing to accept it, because it was not as I expected. I felt that I had denied the Lord that gave it to me. I thought my doom was sealed, and that I was as sure of hell as though I was already there. I was sure I had committed the unpardonable sin. My parents became alarmed about me. I wrung my hands in agony and despair. No one could make me think that there could ever be any mercy for me.

One of the deacons came in and began to sing:

"Saw ye my Saviour?"

It distressed me dreadfully. I am certain there is no singing in hell. I spent that dreadful night without rest or sleep. A lady tried until four o'clock in the morning to convince me that there was still hope in my case; but it was unavailing. I determined never to eat again, but to go to hell from that bed. Oh, the agony of a lost soul! My parents came into my room, and said I must get up. They helped me to rise, but I could neither walk nor eat. I was helpless. A lady, after conversing with me, said: "Take the Bible, and go into your room; perhaps the Lord will meet you there." Just then I thought I would do so. I kneeled down and tried to ask God, just once more, to save me. I told the Lord, if he pleased to save me I would be saved; otherwise I must perish. I there surrendered all to God, and trusted in him. That moment he accepted me. I loved the Lord, and he loved me.

I opened the Bible, and the first words I saw were: "Peace be unto you." Then I knew for myself that I was converted. Christians looked so lovely. I did not know the season of the year till that moment, and when I looked out of the window and saw the trees in bloom, every blossom and blade of grass seemed to be praising God. That evening I walked two miles up Sharon mountain to an evening meeting, and home again.

I soon united with the Baptist Church in Cornwall. That was forty-seven years ago. I tried to live a devoted Christian life, but did not think it possible in those days to be sanctified until death.

About fourteen years ago, we lived in Mount Morris, N. Y. A sister in the church professed to enjoy the blessing of sanctification. I asked her if it was instantaneous or progressive? She answered, "Both." I concluded if it was for her, it was for me. I had thought it was a *Methodist* doctrine, but to my astonishment I found it was a *Bible* doctrine. I could hardly open the Bible without feeling the obligation to be holy. I felt I must come out from the world, and love God with all my heart. I was striving for the blessing about seven months, under deep, pungent conviction.

One day a Congregational minister was preaching on the doctrine of sanctification, and I was listening most attentively. When he was about half through his sermon, my load of sin was taken away in an instant. I felt as if newly converted. I had my first love again. I possessed perfect peace. All was right between God and my soul. I wanted nothing. God could do nothing wrong.

I felt that I launched out from the shore; that I was set in a large room, and my feet stood in an even place. I enjoyed Christ more than ever. I lived above the world.

I did not tell my experience until about six months afterward, when I related it to my pastor. He said: "Sister T., you will have to confess that, some time." But the tempter said: "Keep still; don't tell of it, until you see if you can live it." Alas! I listened to his suggestion, and, as a consequence, I lost the blessing.

But, having once enjoyed the sweet rest of faith, I felt that I could not live without it, and I began again to seek the blessing of a clean heart. I found it much harder than before. One day I was alone, praying. A light shone into my heart, and I saw all that was there. I detected conformity to the world, back-sliding and self-seeking. I thought I had consecrated all to God long before this. But the sight of the filth I then discovered in my heart astonished me. I prayed earnestly for ten days, but still carried the dreadful load of sin.

One morning I awoke long before daylight, and commenced to pray in great earnest, determined to wrestle until I died, unless God would remove my awful load of iniquity. After I had agonized for one hour, I felt some relief. This encouraged me, and I continued to pray for about another hour, when all my sin was taken away, and Jesus appeared to me "the brightness of the Father's glory, and the express image of his person." He was close to me. I seemed to go out of myself and into Christ. I saw that my heart was cleansed from all unrighteousness. I cried, I laughed, and praised the Lord aloud. Oh, the peace that I enjoyed; the consciousness of a clean heart, and "peace that passeth all understanding."

I was not now slow to confess the blessing. All I wanted was hearers. Christ has held me just so for years. I enjoy the rest of faith. I live in the land of Beulah, where the flowers bloom the year round, and the sun goes not down. The blood of Jesus cleanses my soul from all sin. I am now sixty-eight years old, and will soon pass over the river. Heart purity is what we need in the church.

EXPERIENCE OF BROTHER J. H. S.,

OF NEW HAVEN, CONN.

I WAS the child of Christian parents, my father being a minister of the gospel, and was early instructed in religious truth, and became familiar with the Holy Scriptures. I was naturally very conscientious, and, at the age of ten or eleven years, thought I was converted, and took part in religious meetings. I lost this experience, however, and, in my fifteenth year, being forced by changed circumstances to go out into the world alone to support myself, away from home and its influences, I strayed far from the path of rectitude, and grew up to manhood in the indulgence of vicious habits, and seemed in great danger of ruining both body and soul. I used intoxicating liquors freely, neglected the house of God, desecrated the Sabbath, and entertained skeptical opinions—associating, of course, with others of like habits. I was followed all this time, however, by a mother's prayers and faithful exhortations.

At about the age of twenty-three, I formed, in the providence of God, an attachment for a young Christian lady, who afterwards became my wife. The effect of this new emotion was, under God's blessing, to soften my heart, draw me away from my vicious habits, and revive the religious impressions of early years. I began to attend public worship regularly, and at last felt that I ought not to become the head of a family, without first becoming a Christian. With this conviction I knelt down one evening in the fall of 1856, and dedicated myself to the service of my heavenly Father. This change was not preceded by any acute conviction of sin, nor succeeded by any emotions of peace and joy, such as frequently accompany conversion. I immediately commenced to attend and take part in devotional meetings, and soon after became a member of the First Baptist Church of New Haven, being baptized upon profession of my faith.

For about two years I was very active in the church, but felt a growing consciousness of the sinfulness of my heart, such as I had not felt before making a profession of religion. I became greatly dissatisfied with myself, and with other Christians; began to indulge erroneous views, gave up prayer, neglected the ordinances of the church, and for several years lived a most unsettled and unhappy life, so far as religious convictions were concerned, although I thought and read much upon the subject.

In the summer of 1865, Bro. A. B. Earle held a series of meetings in New Haven, during which time many were added to the church, and God in great mercy brought me to his fold again. I acknowledged my errors, was restored to the church, and, with a chastened spirit, endeavored faithfully to discharge the duties and live the life of a Christian. I still felt, however, the bondage of an evil heart of unbelief, and the power of besetting sins. "When I would do good, evil was present with me," and my cry frequently was, "Oh, wretched man that I am, who shall deliver me from the body of this death?" I resolved and re-resolved; I prayed, and wept, and struggled, only to be overcome again and again. I read in the Scriptures of another and better experience—one of joy, victory, and self-sacrifice, but I did not understand it, nor had I the remotest idea how to obtain it.

I lived in this way until February, 1868, when Bro. John Q. Adams commenced a series of meetings in New Haven, preaching, in the rooms of the Young Men's Christian Association, a course of afternoon sermons upon "Sanctification." I was very much prejudiced against him, having seen, as I thought, an end of all perfection. Business engagements, also, prevented my attending many of his sermons upon this special subject, but I became deeply interested in the few I heard. My soul longed for rest. In one of the evening meetings I arose with others in token of a new consecration. I was thoroughly in earnest. The following afternoon I heard a sermon from Bro. Adams, on temptation, which removed many difficulties from my mind, and the next day I found myself in the possession of a new, distinct, and happy experience, such as I had never before known. I could no more deny it than I could my own existence. My soul was lifted as on wings. I felt that the Comforter had come. How he entered, I could not say; but this I knew, he was in my heart.

With this joyous emotion came a distinct and certain apprehension, also new to me, of the Lord Jesus Christ, as my righteousness and sanctification. I believed with the heart that his blood cleansed me from all sin; that he bore *all* my sins in his own body on the tree, and in this confidence I have ever since rejoiced. There have been seasons of comparative darkness, many of fierce temptations, but out of them all hath the Lord delivered me. I find the path grows brighter and clearer, and my faith stronger, and feel that "for me to live is Christ;" that I am no longer under condemnation, but have received the spirit of adoption by which I am enabled to say in child-like confidence, Abba, Father.

I heartily and entirely renounce all trust in anything that I can do or feel as a ground of acceptance with God, but have an abiding trust in the suffering and death of our Lord Jesus Christ, as a full and complete atonement for all my sin, and as restoring me fully to his favor. I have a strong and growing love for my Saviour, giving me a supreme desire to please him in all things, great or small, and feel a peculiar pleasure in yielding to his will in occasions naturally trying to the flesh. I feel a strong attachment for all who love our Lord Jesus Christ, of whatever name or nation, or whatever their progress in Christian life. I cherish a great and increasing desire for the salvation of sinners. I exercise a firm trust in God for matters temporal as well as spiritual, and rejoice in hope of the glory of God.

I close this relation of my experience, almost ashamed of having attempted it, for I feel that I am an unprofitable servant, and have done only that which it was my duty to do, and do not desire that any one should look at me, or the exercises of my mind, but unto JESUS. I have only written it, in the hope that some weak or doubting disciple may be led to look away from self, and behold with believing eyes the Lamb of God that *taketh away* the sin of the world, and be enabled with the whole heart to exclaim: "My Lord and my God."

EXPERIENCE OF L. R.,

A BROTHER IN INDIANA.

In early life I was often seriously impressed with the need of an interest in the Saviour, but, like other youths, drowned my convictions and mingled with the vain. Hearing faithful sermons from time to time, I was led to vow obedience to the commands of God, and promised at such times to seek the favor of the Lord; but, when I was reminded of my promise, I was not ready. The Lord bore with me year after year; and oh, what a mercy that I was not left to myself.

I was married at an early age, and, when we first commenced house-keeping, solemn thoughts rushed into my mind. Well do I remember when we sat at our own table for the first time, how I felt the duty I owed to God, and the need of his help and blessing to commence aright. The preaching of the word often made me feel deeply solemn; still, for months there was no particular alteration.

In process of time, the little band of Christians,

who then maintained the preaching of the gospel a part of the time, began to talk about building a house for the Lord. I began to feel animated with the hope of their success, and after they commenced the work, all that summer I felt a peculiar interest in the welfare and prosperity of that little Baptist Church. I felt, during the time of building, that there would be a revival of religion, and expressed the same. The summer passed away, autumn came, the house was completed and opened for worship. It was dedicated, and the young man chosen to be the pastor was ordained the same day. All was solemn and interesting to me. A few weeks passed away, and the little church received a new impulse. They soon began to talk of a four-days' meeting, this being in those times when four-days' meetings were often held and blessed. I was pleased to hear the announcement of that meeting, and at once resolved to attend it. I gave up all, and placed myself in the sanctuary. I listened to all that was said, but still felt my heart hard from day to day. My greatest desire was that I might see my sins as I thought I must, and this was all my prayer, but still I could not feel.

As I lay on my bed one night, pleading that

God would show me my sins, suddenly it seemed that I heard a shrill voice saying, "Sinner, look before you." It then seemed to me that I saw hell opened before me, but I will not try to describe the scenes that were presented to my view. After this my feelings were more intense, and, as the fourth day had now come, it seemed to me, if the meetings closed, and I did not find peace, it would be the last call to me. This heightened my distress, and I prayed with earnestness; so passed the day. I went to my home from the church, it being near dark, and I felt very much depressed in mind. I knew not what to say or do, but, feeling a desire to go alone and pray, I thought, as I lived only a few rods from church, I would go into the church, it being dark, and no one would see me. I shut the outside door as I went in, also the gallery door after me, and then went where I used to sit in the choir, and knelt on the floor. I was frightened from my knees by a strange noise, and went out of the house thinking, "What shall I do?"

I thought I would go and meet one of the deacons who had talked with me, and tell him my feelings. I started, but the thought came to me, "He can't save me." I stopped and pondered, but again resolved to go and meet him as he would be coming to the evening meeting. I accordingly met him, and talked more freely with him than I had done before. I felt some relief by opening my mind freely to him. We went into the house of the Lord, and took a seat with my wife. I felt feeble in body as in mind, and as my wife was always full of attention to all my wants, and always tried to comfort me in despondency, I turned to her and took her hand in mine. In a few moments this Scripture was presented to my mind: "A man must forsake father and mother, wife and children, for the kingdom of heaven." I let go her hand, and the same instant the Saviour appeared to my view in all his loveliness. I thought I saw him in bodily shape, between the heavens and earth, surrounded with heavenly glory. He extended his hand to me, and said, "Son, thy sins are forgiven." But the next thought was, "Satan has transformed himself into an angel of light," and I feared that he had deceived me. All my convictions were gone, and I tried to pray for conviction again, but could not get it. I could not get any burden on my soul again.

I sat through the exercises of the evening, and could but rejoice, while at the same time I feared; but at the close of the service the invitation was given to all that hoped their sins were forgiven to arise. It was a trying moment to me. I asked myself: "What shall I do? Shall I arise, and deceive the people?" Then again the thought came: "Well, I do hope my sins are forgiven; so, if they are not, it will not be deception in me." So I arose, and gained much strength by so doing; and as I was the first one that indulged hope in that meeting, old Christians soon gathered around me, and, while we lingered in the house of the Lord that evening, it seemed to be filled with heavenly brightness and glory.

I did not sleep much that night, but found myself in the house of the Lord at sunrise the next morning, where the church were gathered for prayer. I was soon on my feet, and my tongue was praising God, while old Christians were weeping and rejoicing. Oh, what a memorable morn was that! What a thrill of joy it gives me this moment to recall its scenes, though thirty-five years have passed. I lived in the sunlight of God's countenance that winter, the most of the time. After a few weeks I felt the duty of baptism enjoined upon me, and, the first Sabbath in January, with two others, I was buried with Christ in baptism. I enjoyed much of the presence of my

Saviour for a long time, but after a few years passed away I began to be disobedient, and indulged in little acts of transgression.

I was not left to neglect the forms of religion, but kept up the family altar, and attended the weekly social meeting, and generally took part in them, and often enjoyed good seasons while there; but how soon, when I was out of the meetings, I gave way to depraved nature. I often thought, "Shall I always live in this frame of mind?" I did long to see a glorious revival of God's work, and sometimes hoped I might be delivered from such a state. Thus I lived for years. I thought of trying to come up on higher ground, and, when I heard any one talk of a full consecration, of full salvation, and of enjoying perfect love, I wished such a state were mine, but had not faith strong enough to believe the promises.

In the latter part of February, 1867, there was held a series of meetings by the church with which I am connected, and the Lord came down in a glorious manner. Such demonstrations of his power and grace are not often felt. The Lord met me there, and I was quite broken down. I wept and cried, and the Lord heard. During the meetings the ministers felt that something more must be done, and called upon all that would to consecrate themselves and all they had anew to God. Such were asked to take a certain position. That moment was a trying one to me. I wanted to comply, and I feared there would be duties to be performed and crosses to bear that I might shrink from; but the Lord gave me strength to take the position, and to give up all to him without reserve, and he accepted the offering.

After this the Lord's blessing was poured out in a glorious manner. My soul was free, and I felt that I could come near to him in and out of meetings. The long-looked-for day had dawned upon my soul when I was made free by the Son of God. I then saw a fulness in Christ that I had not known before. I felt that I was dwelling in Christ, and he in me. Since that time my views have been quite different. The doctrine of entire sanctification, which I had been taught all my days to discard, now looks beautiful, and of all the most desirable and lovely. Oh, how inconsistent it appears to me for a Christian to dwell in any other state.

When that series of meetings closed, and I returned home to mingle with the world, anxious feelings pervaded my whole soul lest I might not live in such a frame of mind. I visited my closet, and there prayed for strength to live near my Saviour. In the morning I took the Bible, read a few verses, and prayed earnestly for strength to live that day free from known sin. I believed, when I asked, that God could and would give me the strength needed, that I might live and walk with him. I found all the aid I sought. The next day I did likewise, and he again met and blessed me abundantly, and so I have lived from day to day in the light of God's countenance.

I feel that I am in Christ as the branch is in the vine. Oh, how wonderful is the love of God. Oh, the depths of the riches of his grace; how unspeakable his great mercies! Since the time referred to, the Saviour has been so near to me that I have had but few evil thoughts arise in my mind, and I have been enabled to banish them at once. The Saviour has not suffered the evil one scarcely to touch me for a number of months past.

Oh, that Christians would awake to this subject, and find there is higher ground for them to occupy. Oh, how great the Christian's privilege, if we will but come up and enjoy it.

EXPERIENCE OF MRS. H. A. R.

WHEN first, by divine grace, I turned my back upon the city of Destruction, and my face toward the Celestial City, I was fully determined to know nothing among men save Jesus Christ and him crucified. I saw before me the straight and narrow way. I saw that it was a rough and thorny path; but I saw at the end the "shining ones" bearing in their hands a brilliant crown—aye, more, I saw Jesus, the Sun of righteousness, beaming upon the path; and, laying aside every weight, I joyfully exclaimed, "I will run this race, blessed Jesus, looking unto thee!"

For weeks and months I lived in joy unspeakable, with this my only motto: "For me to live is Christ." But, alas! I knew not then that it was the Christian's privilege to be holy in this life. There came frequent seasons of depression, and darkness, when I groaned under the power of sin. The promise, "Sin shall not have dominion over you," I thought the sweetest of all the promises of God's word; yet I knew not that it meant a present deliverance from sin. I rested sweetly in Jesus as my justification; I knew the robe of his spotless righteousness was upon me. I had often heard his sweet voice saying unto me: "Thou art all fair, my love, there is no spot in thee;" but while I rejoiced in my clean, white, sinless robe, received by faith alone, I saw not Jesus in all his fulness as a complete Saviour from all sin. Not yet was he made unto me *sanctification*. Perfection was my aim; but it loomed before me, a dizzy height to which I thought to *attain*.

For several years, I went on, sometimes repining, sometimes cast down, and often groaning with the apostle: "Wretched being that I am, who shall deliver me from the body of this death?" Yet I could not, like him, "thank God, through Jesus Christ." Oh! the weariness of my soul; how often were my eyes turned with restless longings toward the dark river, which I thought alone would bring deliverance and rest for my weary soul. Thus years went on, the way growing darker and more difficult, and the way of holiness more distant and hopeless than ever. Occasionally, I caught glimpses of a "higher life." I felt there was something better for the Christian, even in this life, than to "go mourning all the day long." I heard, I read of this highway of holiness, yet thought not, nor hoped, that I might walk therein. I became discouraged; the darkness of unbelief covered my soul, and one night, being far distant from Christian friends, and surrounded by worldliness and folly, having yielded to temptation and compromised with the world, when I retired to my room, oh, how fearful was the darkness which filled my soul, and crushed me to the very depths. Before me loomed the height which for so many years I had been striving to attain; and then how fearfully I realized that I was sitting at its base, with broken resolutions, misspent time, wasted talents, spreading out in wide desolation before me, and amid them all a Saviour crucified afresh, his holy eyes filled with tender reproof.

Oh, how bitter were my self-upbraidings that night. Satan stood near me saying, "It is of no use; give up trying; it is impossible to lead a holy life in this world;" and my soul said: "I will give up; I cannot attain to it;" and thus utter hopelessness took possession of me. Then worldly hopes and worldly schemes and worldly ambitions filled my heart, and with these husks I sought to satisfy its longings, and found how vain, how hopeless the attempt. My broken vows, my cowardly abandonment of the cause of Jesus, constantly rose before me, and I found no peace; my soul would be satisfied with nothing less than God. Then came letters from a dear friend who had found the rest of faith, which showed me the way of holiness by simple trust in Jesus. But then I was too full of worldly thoughts and ambitions to desire it. The world was smiling upon me, offering its choicest joys for my acceptance, and my eager heart exclaimed: "Here is happiness! here is joy!" I stretched forth my hands to grasp the prize, when, with one single stroke, the cup was dashed from my lips. The future was shrouded in deepest gloom, and the present seemed hopeless. I understood it. I recognized in that fearful trial the hand of God; but, oh! how bitterly my soul rebelled. I then learned that it was truly "an evil and a bitter thing to forsake the Lord."

Another year passed on, a year of hopelessness and restlessness. Although Jesus had stripped me of everything that he might give me himself, I refused to receive him: my heart cried continually after its idols, when, by his wonderful providence, I was again brought back to my early home, and among the dear Christian friends with whom I had walked in the days of my "first love." Then the blessed doctrine of sanctification by faith was constantly before me. I saw exemplifications of it in the lives of loved friends, but my soul was much depressed because I had so long rejected this light, and I thought God would not now give it me. I was greatly troubled; my past unfaithfulness rose up to reproach me, and Satan tempted me to unbelief. Oh! how my soul was tossed and sometimes overwhelmed. I said, "There is no hope." Then again I caught such glimpses of the beauty and glory of this way, that I was enabled to make an entire consecration of myself to Jesus. "Take me, my Saviour, just as I am, vile, with all my past unfaithfulness and sinfulness rising like a mountain to crush me; take me, I am thine, wholly thine, body, soul, and spirit; all I have, and all I am is thine, wholly, forever thine."

Then my soul found some rest — but oh, how Satan raged. He scarcely left me for a moment. How he tempted me to unbelief; and often I feared that God had indeed forsaken me. I knew that I deserved to be forsaken, yet, in spite of all, Jesus held me up, and with naked faith I trusted in him. I learned then what it meant to "walk by faith;" for at times a horror of darkness was upon me. The first ray of light gleamed into my soul when I first arose to make confession of my faith in Jesus as a complete Saviour. I had then received no sensible evidence of my acceptance, but I clung to Jesus and rested on his word only, by simple faith. After I had made this confession, Jesus drew near me.

That night as I lay upon my bed, communing with my heart and struggling against the suggestions of Satan, who now seemed enraged because of the confession I had made, and which he had been trying with all his might to keep me from making, Jesus whispered, "Thou art mine," and I closed my eyes in peace, resting upon this sweet word. But with the next morning came the same darkness, the same struggles, the same temptations. Thus two weeks passed away, during which I walked by faith alone, without any evidence that the offering which I had made was accepted, save the naked word of God, while Satan constantly tempted me to unbelief.

When I went one afternoon to the meeting for the advancement of this blessed truth, my soul was much depressed. I had been crying all the day long: "Jesus, save me; Jesus, save me;" and Satan seemed more than ever determined to have me. But, glory to our strong Saviour, I was delivered; for while there I received glorious evidence that I was saved. A flood of light gleamed through my soul, and peace like a river flowed therein. I felt then the power of Jesus' blood to cleanse from all sin. I was complete in him. He was made unto me *sanctification*. My weary soul was at rest. It was as though I had been taken off my feet in the midst of my fruitless struggles to climb the mount, and placed upon the summit in the full enjoyment of the glowing prospect, and pure, delightful air. Oh, how sweetly my soul rested. Then I learned what it was to *believe* and enter into rest. "My beloved is mine and I am his."

I am coming up out of the wilderness, leaning upon the arm of my beloved. Worldly riches, worldly honors, worldly ease and pleasure, how ye sink into insignificance before his sweet presence. My soul tramples on the best thou canst present. Jesus is my present and everlasting portion. Jesus, in whom dwelleth all the fulness of the Godhead bodily, *is mine*—mine, in all his fulness; and I am his. He himself is the glorious altar which sanctifies even this vile offering. My soul is set free. Sin has not dominion over me, for Jesus, like a mighty conqueror, has broken its power, and has taken full possession, where once it abounded.

Here is rest for the weary, sin-tossed soul—Jesus, the present Saviour of his people. Come to him, all ye that labor and are heavy laden, and he will give you *rest*. Words cannot express the significance of this one word *rest*. Only those whose souls have been tossed and wearied by the cruel power of sin and Satan, and who have found deliverance by the blood of Jesus, can know what it means. "We who believe do enter into rest." Glory be to Jesus! I have entered in, and my soul is at rest.

EXPERIENCE OF MISS LIZZIE M.

I DO not remember the time when I did not desire truly to be a Christian. At the age of twelve I followed Christ in baptism. I felt conscious that I had given myself away, and now I must take up every cross that presented itself. I was a constant attendant on the prayer-meeting, and often heard older Christians excuse themselves when called upon to pray, and then turn to me, a child, and place this heavy cross before me. How my nature shrank! The still small voice would say: "Ashamed of Jesus?" and then I dared not refuse to try. Tremblingly I would attempt and falter; then the tempter would assail me, trying to mortify my pride. How I longed for counsel; how I wept and prayed that I might do all my Father's will. I seemed to grope in darkness.

The experiences of older Christians were a stumbling-block to me. I did not dare to believe or to feel that the promises were indeed mine. I well recollect hearing an aged Christian constantly say, as he arose to speak: "Well, *if* I know my own heart, I *think* I am a Christian." When I would whisper, Job says: "I *know* that my Redeemer liveth," "Ah!" the tempter would say, "that was for Job. Look! these old Christians dare not say they believe. What presumption for you to say you *know* that you belong to Jesus!"

Thus years passed in struggling and fighting, striving to bear the cross that seemed so heavy to bear, yet feeling constantly that I might say: Jesus is mine. Duties were borne, hoping that some day light might dawn. I thought I was happy. I knew that God had often blessed me, and I praised him; but there was something more I desired. My soul was *not* satisfied. It longed to drink deeper of that fountain flowing so freely.

About this time my attention was drawn toward the conversion of my Sunday-school class. None knew the Lord, so I vowed to him that if he would give to me the conversion of my class as a token that I was truly the Lord's, thenceforth I would devote my life to his service. My prayer was answered. I then felt assured that henceforth my life was not my own. Duties presented themselves. The cross looked so weighty, how could I take it up? The vow would seem as if it were registered upon my heart. While I did not doubt I was the Lord's, why this weight? How often did I cry in agony unto the Lord that he would reveal himself so to me, that this trembling would cease when I attempted to speak or pray when called upon.

One day a dear sister, speaking in a prayer-circle, said: "Oh, it is such a privilege for me to speak of the love of Jesus; I wish I could see a cross in it." I looked at her with wonder. Can it be possible for her? Then Jesus can give it to me. I soon became interested in a little circle of prayer, who met to talk about the way that Jesus was leading them, and to seek for a baptism of holiness, that they might draw nearer to God. This was just what my soul needed. I felt strengthened as I met with them from week to week. I found I must come out of self, and wholly rest on Jesus to do it all. I must be willing, if needs be, to stand alone and make a venture for the Lord, relying wholly upon him for strength, and by simple *faith* commit *all* into his hands. His will must be mine, and I must be nothing.

Light broke into my mind. I saw the rock upon which for so long a time my soul had been resting. I obeyed instantly the still small voice, as I heard it bidding me *to duty*, not questioning, as formerly, what would be the result. I had only to obey, Jesus would take care of the result. The trembling *ceased, the cross vanished*. The privilege seemed *so great* to labor for Christ, I eagerly embraced every opportunity to use every talent for my Master; and oh, the sweet peace that has constantly been mine!

As I look back I am amazed, and long to tell all of this loving Saviour. I feel daily that he is indeed leading me, and often gives to me such tokens of love in answer to prayer, that I feel I am talking to a friend face to face. Then came this lonely feeling: "Few appreciate this inner life; few understand it, and oft misinterpret it." Then, amid the opposition from cold professors, that so often nip the buds just as they begin to blossom, I would seem to see the pitying eye of Jesus as he looked so grieved and said: "What, will you also go away?"

Trembling one! this joy may be your constant, abiding guest. Be not satisfied until you can say: I know in whom I believe. Go forth, holding on to the strong arm of Jesus. Though the waves beat high against you, stand firm, looking unto Jesus, and you are safe. Look upon the Christian duties of life as blessed opportunities to labor for Jesus. Then, at last, around God's throne his jewels will all be gathered in, and we shall stand clothed in the spotless robe of Christ's righteousness.

EXPERIENCE OF L. M. W.,

STEWARD OF THE "BAND OF FAITH" IN SHURTLEFF COLLEGE, ILLINOIS.

I was converted to Christ about ten years ago, and after my conversion I enjoyed the love of Jesus for some months, as most young converts do. At the time of my conversion I had a small farm, and, after looking the matter all over, I concluded I had enough of this world; so I told the Lord that whatever he gave me more than a living, I would devote to benevolent objects. This promise, by his grace, I have kept.

But all this time I had not learned to trust Christ as a Saviour from all sin. In spite of all my efforts to the contrary, I would at times get angry, and consequently lose my religious enjoyment—not thinking of my dear Jesus for half a day at a time. I did not take time to read the Bible as I should, and my poor soul was starved. My work drove the body and starved the soul.

I was looking forward to death as the dear

friend that should deliver me from the power of sin. But while attending the anniversaries in St. Louis, in May, 1865, I learned, from the experience of others, that Jesus could save from all sin now. I searched the Bible, and found that it confirmed the precious truth. I went home from the meetings and emptied my heart all out, and thought I would pick its contents all over—select the good, and throw the bad away. I found it to be all bad, but I knew the precious Jesus could cleanse and sanctify it all. I brought all to him, as the altar that sanctifieth the gift, and then I knew that he was able to save to the uttermost.

From that time until now, Jesus has kept me in perfect peace, because my mind is stayed on him. Many times the night has been dark and stormy, but, with "Christ in the vessel," it has been all peace within my soul. He is my constant companion. I go to bed with him, and wake up with him. He is always at hand to help or give counsel in trouble. He is my present and perfect Saviour, and his blood cleanseth me from all sin. To his name be all the glory!

EXPERIENCE OF MRS. C. H. PUTNAM,

A MEMBER OF THE FIRST BAPTIST CHURCH, NEW YORK CITY.

MY first consciousness of spiritual life was a sense of want; an inward void, which the most zealous pursuit of worldly pleasure failed to satisfy. This anxious grasping of the soul after an unknown good was at length met in a manner both singular and mysterious.

Religion became the only subject of interest, and I began to read the Bible, of which I was ignorant as any heathen. There I found the doctrine of the *new birth;* that I must "be born again;" and earnestly I set forth to understand and obtain this state of regeneration. Thinking that this change was insisted on as a pre-requisite for entering the kingdom of heaven, and also that forgiveness of sins was through the death of Christ, I hence inferred the following theory of salvation:

That sinners were pardoned for Christ's sake, and were accepted, and finally saved upon being *born again;* this last act giving them a title as children to the heavenly inheritance.

It was the evidence of this change of heart, and the features which I could discover in myself of being a child of God, upon which really rested my hope, while my confession of that hope took the form used by others, that I "trust in Christ for salvation." I could not doubt that I had experienced a change, and in that change I rested, secretly and unconsciously believing that I was, by reason of this change, acceptable to God, and regarded with favor by him, and that if I properly maintained and faithfully improved the stock of grace which was imparted to me, I should keep myself in his favor, and become in due time a great and strong Christian. But, to my great surprise and mortification, it was just the contrary. I became weaker daily and less satisfied with myself, because I seemed constantly to be falling more and more short of the standard which I had set up in my mind as the mark at which I must aim. I was greatly discouraged, but yet pressed on, laboring like a galley-slave, first at this and then at that supposed hindrance in my way to holiness, yet never once imagining that I was not "striving lawfully" to win the prize.

After I had been thus toiling for nearly a year, the Lord was graciously pleased to open my eyes to a new discovery, viz., that the grace of God was bestowed *freely for Christ's sake without regard to the personal merit of the object.* Yet so deep-rooted was the idea that I must become better before Christ could receive me, that I listened with solicitude bordering on despair to all that fell from the lips of Christians, lest they should contradict the *life-giving truth*, and make it appear, after all, that I did not rightly understand the Scriptures. I was constantly perplexed in trying to reconcile this discovery with my preconceived notions of the believer's growth in grace. I had been taught to consider this growth as dependent on the faithfulness and diligence with which I improved upon the stock which I supposed to be imparted in regeneration, and which I was to add to, and also to draw from, in any emergency of duty or temptation. There was a vague idea that the Holy Spirit had something to do with this work, and that by his aid (which I should enjoy if I did my own part) I was to grow daily more holy, and more deserving of the divine favor, until I arrived at the stature of a strong and perfect Christian character. This was my theory of *sanctification*, founded in human reason, and confirmed by the religious teaching which I then enjoyed. Greatly was I puzzled to reconcile it with my daily experience; but, as in duty bound, I always attributed the difficulty to my own unfaithfulness, and would go to work again with firm determination to be more watchful and diligent in future. But, alas! I grew none the better, but rather the worse. The little strength I had was becoming weaker and weaker, while the sins of the flesh—the corruptions of my nature—were gaining ground, and threatened to take the entire field. In this state of things there remained but one reasonable conclusion, which was, that I was mistaken in the whole, and never had any grace.

It was in this way that the first five years of my Christian course was spent, toiling, like a galley-slave, to obtain something which eluded my grasp, and left me fluctuating between hope and fear. It was the discovery of Christ, that I have above related, which swept away, at one stroke, the baseless fabric I had been trying to build, and explained the meaning of the apostle when he said: "I glory in infirmity, that Christ's own power may rest upon me."

I now enjoyed a comfortable frame of mind, though still harassed and buffeted by the law of my members, which strove hard to keep me weak in the faith. And still more was I stumbled by the preaching which I was in the habit of hearing. This was of a character to nourish and keep alive the struggle of self-righteousness by placing Christian duty and obedience as the cause and foundation of our enjoying the divine favor, the degree of which was consequently measured by our faithfulness and diligence.

There was one manifestation with which I was favored at this period which I cannot forbear to mention, though from its very remarkable nature I have sometimes been tempted to be silent in regard to it, lest I should be accused of enthusiasm or presumption. Never, in the darkest season of outward or inward conflict (and they both have been many), have I been tempted to call in question what I then experienced.

I had long enjoyed a sweet nearness to God in prayer, and felt ardent desire to be unreservedly consecrated to his service. In one of these seasons he was pleased to seal to my soul, in a new and indescribable manner, its interest in the great covenant of redemption, making over to my use and benefit all the riches of grace and glory which are embraced in that covenant. I have said it was indescribable, and truly it was so; *not capable of being explained, or even comprehended, but by those who have experienced something similar.* The ardent thirst for self-consecration which he had implanted in my soul was met and accepted, as was also an unreserved transfer of all that I could call mine. In this I seemed as if *wholly passive*, and at the same time mightily and mysteriously active. The persons of the Sacred Trinity—Father, Son, and Holy Spirit—seemed unitedly and yet distinctively, each in his own peculiar office, covenanting to be mine—to pardon, redeem, and sanctify. Everlasting faithfulness and love stood pledged in my behalf, and Jehovah himself said to my soul: "Fear not, for I have redeemed thee; when thou passest through the waters I will be with thee, and through the rivers, they shall not overflow thee; when thou walkest through the fire, thou shalt not be burnt, neither shall the flame kindle upon thee." My happy soul was full—was satisfied; I could ask no more.

This manifestation was altogether so different from anything I ever before experienced that it seemed to constitute a new and important era in my existence. Its effect upon my mind was lasting and vivid; I was no longer *my own*, and when

I prayed for my husband and children, it was with the feeling that all I had was the Lord's. Often before had I felt the *desire* in my heart thus to relinquish all, and leave myself and my interests in his hands; but not till now did it seem *done;* never did I experience anything like what I now felt. In the perfect and finished work of Christ, I felt myself saved with an "everlasting salvation." He was made unto me "wisdom, righteousness, sanctification, and redemption;" and in him was the fulness of all that I could conceive or desire of good.

I was next led to understand the office-work or the Holy Spirit; that this divine agent is emphatically the glorifier of Jesus; that he "does not speak of himself," or of his own work in the heart, but leads the believer to look away from all that is *wrought in him,* as well as all that is *done by him,* to the perfect work and complete salvation of the Saviour. His whole aim is to exalt and magnify the Lord Jesus Christ by taking of the things that are his and showing them to the eye of faith, so as to destroy all confidence in the flesh, and cause it to rest only, and rejoice only in the Lord.

The entire ministry of the Holy Spirit, also, is to honor and glorify both Father and Son, by opening and revealing the mysteries of grace as recorded in the written word, according to the prayer of Jesus, when he prays for his people: "Sanctify them through the truth; thy word is truth."

I had been taught that *sanctification* was not to be included in the perfect robe of the Redeemer's righteousness; that it was the gradual work of the Holy Spirit in the heart, and consequently was incomplete in this life. But the gracious Comforter, the Spirit of truth, now enabled me to see that this was a meagre and partial view of the subject; that sanctification or deliverance from sin was, in Scripture, attributed equally to the Father, the Son, and the Holy Spirit. As the work of the Father, it consists in choosing and setting apart in Christ the whole elect family or church of the first-born, predestinating them to be conformed to the image of his Son. As the work of Christ, it consists in his setting himself apart to the work of redemption, in which work they, as *one with him*, their representative head, are "perfected forever," "circumcised" (or crucified) with him, in putting off the body of sin, so that they are, in him, delivered from sin, and dead to it as he is dead. As the work of the Holy Spirit, *sanctification* consists in giving the believer a spiritual discernment of "the things of God," turning away the veil of unbelief, and presenting such a discovery of Christ, in his offices of Prophet, Priest, and King, as shall humble the pride of the carnal heart, show him his own utter nothingness and dependence, and enable him to "rejoice in Christ Jesus, having no confidence in the flesh." By this work he is gradually transformed into the image of Christ, by every new discovery being made "to grow up into him," until, at death, he shall be "like him, because '*he shall see him as he is.*'"

Fifty years of my life have thus been spent in a gradual "coming to the light." "Slow of heart to believe," and accept the great "things which God has laid up for them that fear him," they have always opened upon me by surprise, confounding my unbelief, and filling me with wonder and admiration at "the heights and depths, the lengths and breadths, of the love of Christ, which passeth knowledge." Growing hungry and thirsty by that which it feeds upon, my soul has been brought to feel that, marvellous as is the grace manifested in the *imparted* benefits, the gifts and blessings received *from* the Lord of life and glory, yet nothing short of *himself*—a *personal* in-dwelling Christ—can wholly satisfy its desires or meet its necessities. "I will not leave you comfortless; I will come unto you and make my abode with you." Even so, Lord; let me realize that thou dwellest in me, that thou abidest in me, and I in thee, vitally and inseparably; in my weakness be thou my resting-place, and "what time I am afraid," let me shelter under the shadow of thy wings. While I sojourn in the wilderness, "feed me according to the integrity of thy heart, and guide me by the skilfulness of thy hand;" and, dying to all things else, let me live only to thee.

EXPERIENCE OF A BAPTIST MINISTER'S WIFE.

MY parents were godly people, members of the Congregational church, and instructed their children in the first principles of religion and their duty to God. I was, therefore, from my earliest recollection, a subject of serious impressions, but never indulged the hope that my sins were pardoned until about the age of fourteen years; and even then I could not tell the exact time when Christ spake peace to my soul. This fact was a hindrance, for several years, to my progress in the divine life; but I finally learned that the question was not, What *have* I been? but, What *am* I? Am I serving God *now?* If I am his disciple now, it matters not when I became one. Thus the tempter was foiled in his attempt to overthrow my faith.

Soon after my conversion I united with the church to which my parents belonged. But, after struggling against convictions for six years, I at length yielded, and united with a Baptist church. That was a new era in my spiritual life. From that day there was a greater change in my feelings than I had ever known before. I enjoyed very much of the presence of my Saviour from time to time, although I still felt that I had not reached the Bible standard; but I heard nothing of a higher life from Christians for several years.

At length some works on holiness were placed within my reach, and I availed myself of the privilege of reading them. I then saw that it was possible for me, *even me*, to walk in the "highway of holiness." I sought and obtained the blessing of sanctification, and for several months was enabled to trust in Jesus as my Saviour—*my perfect Saviour*. But, not being fully instructed in the way, faith wavered, and I fell. I did not walk in darkness *much* in the years that followed, yet felt many times that I was living far beneath my privilege; although to the praise of God I can say that I received many precious answers to prayer, both for temporal and spiritual blessings.

In the winter of 1865-6, my attention was again called to the subject of holiness, and I determined again to make the consecration, and seek the blessing. Week after week passed away, and still I received no light. One evening after reading the tracts entitled, "The Experience of a Baptist Minister," and of a "Once Fashionable Young Lady," the thought arose: Why do I not enter into this rest? I know it is attainable, and I long for holiness of heart. I trust I was enabled fully to count the cost. The subject was made more clear to me, and I again made the consecration, feeling that I could not leave the room until the victory had been won. I had all the time before been looking for the evidence of acceptance before I believed. I told the Lord now I would hold on by faith and believe even without any sensible evidence. He took me at my word. I did believe that the offering was accepted, though I had no evidence except the written word. Yet I held on by faith, and though I had no ecstatic joys, I possessed sweet peace and confidence in God.

I find that the once aching void is filled, and I can say that Jesus is mine and I am his; and "though he slay me, yet will I trust in him." I am now not my own. My time, my talents, my all, belong to God. Oh that he may enable me to use all to promote his glory! This is all I ask: to know more of Jesus—to be perfectly conformed to him.

> "Blessed Jesus, unto thee
> Evermore the praise shall be."

EXPERIENCE OF MRS. M. A. S.

AT a very early age I was convicted of sin, and sought and found pardon through the merits of Christ. For a time, I walked in the light of his countenance, but finally fell in with the customs of the day, and became lukewarm and formal. I tried to perform my religious duties, and hoped to reach heaven at last. Thus I lived twenty-five years. Then the judgments of God came upon me. He took my eldest daughter, my idol. Then I was led to examine my heart. I found rebellion there. I could not offer the Lord's Prayer. How could I say, "Thy will be done," and not mean it? for I knew that God required truth in the inward parts.

Oh! the anguish of my poor heart at that hour! My loved one gone, and my heart not right in the sight of God. I tried to pray, but the thought would arise, "Give up your will to Christ." This I could not do of myself, and I did not know how to go to Jesus. I knew there was a higher state of religion than I had attained—a place where I could say, "Thy will be done." Some said it was not an instantaneous work, but that I would reach it by-and-by. This did not satisfy me. I felt that help must soon come, or I should die. Some friends advised me to take boarders, thinking to divert my mind in that way. I did so, but no relief came. I held on to God with a trembling hand, and would not let him go. At times I would pray all night for the Lord to give me light. I did not consult my pastor, lest he should think I was not converted, and I did not wish to lessen his confidence in me.

It pleased the Lord, in his wise providence, to send Dr. R. to this place. I went to hear him preach, and he made the doctrine of sanctification so clear and plain that the wayfaring man, though a fool, need not have erred therein. I began to see that it meant something to give up all for Christ's sake. Dr. R. gave an invitation to all who felt the need of this all-cleansing blood on their hearts, to kneel at the altar. I, with a number of others, went forward. My prayer was: "Oh! give me a clean heart." And, with this experience, I cried from the depths of my soul, "O Lord, what wilt thou have me to do?" Then came the struggle, and the answer,

"Will you pray with your boarders?" for I had excluded my boarders from family worship, through a man-fearing spirit.

I mentioned my trouble to my husband; but he thought it was not necessary to be so particular about so small a matter. But it was no small matter to me.

I felt that I must make a clean work of it. I had to make acknowledgments to my boarders for my omission of duty to them in regard to family prayers; and then I solemnly promised God that I would do my duty.

The next morning the young men joined us in worship; and, as I opened the Bible and read, the light of heaven shone into my heart and on the word, as it never had before. As I knelt in prayer, I received such a blessing, that I knew the Lord had lifted his reconciled countenance upon me, and I was fully justified in his sight. I then went to my room, expecting the blessing of perfect love; but, as I knelt to pray, these words came to me: "Are you going to give Mary to the Lord?" For the Lord had laid his afflicting hand upon my second daughter, and I knew that she must die; and could I say that it was right? I knelt the second time in prayer, but I could not say, "Thy will be done."

I arose from my knees and walked the floor, and, as I looked at my darling child, I thought of Abraham when he offered up his *only* son; and I fell upon my face and cried, " Lord, here is Mary; and here is every child I have; and here is my husband; and here I am; and if I become a perfect beggar on the streets, only give me full salvation." Then the power came down, and I was fully saved from everything on this earth. I have been walking in this glorious way for ten years, and to-day I feel this all-cleansing blood on my heart. Praise the Lord forever!

www.ingramcontent.com/pod-product-compliance
Lightning Source LLC
Chambersburg PA
CBHW032103220426
43664CB00008B/1121